Gideon: Wimp to Warrior

Bible Character Series

Robert Lloyd Russell

Published by Robert Lloyd Russell, 2024.

Also by Robert Lloyd Russell

Bible Character Series
Samson: Spirit-Controlled to Self-Centered
Peter: Failure to Faith
Joseph: Victim to Victor
Gideon: Wimp to Warrior

Christian Concepts Series
God's Church: Christ's Pearl
God's Nature: Sonlight Sunlight
God's Child: Like a Tree

Christian Growth Series
God's Desire: How To Please God
God's Light: How To Respond
Christ's Disciple: How To Finish Strong

Christian Theology Series
Christ's Blood: 7+ Amazing Benefits

Pride: Good and Bad
Temptation: 50+ Tips

Missions
Jim Elliot: Recorded Messages

Watch for more at www.booksrlr.com.

Table of Contents

While every precaution has been taken in the preparation of this book, the publisher assumes no responsibility for errors or omissions, or for damages resulting from the use of the information contained herein.

GIDEON: Wimp to Warrior

2024 September 14

Written by Robert Lloyd Russell

Copyright © 2024 Robert Lloyd Russell

Website: BOOKSrlr

Unless otherwise noted Scripture quotations are from:

ESV ~ Scripture quotations are from The Holy Bible, English Standard Version® (ESV®), copyright © 2001 by Crossway, a publishing ministry of Good News Publishers. Used by permission. All rights reserved.

Other Scripture portions as noted are from:

AMP ~ Scripture quotations taken from the Amplified® Bible (AMP), Copyright © 1954, 1958, 1962, 1964, 1965, 1987, 2015 by The Lockman Foundation Used by permission.

BBE ~ The Bible in Basic English, 1949, 1964, public domain.

DRB ~ Douay-Rheims Bible, 1899, public domain.

ESV ~ Scripture quotations are from The Holy Bible, English Standard Version® (ESV®), copyright © 2001 by Crossway, a publishing ministry of Good News Publishers. Used by permission. All rights reserved.

GNT ~ Good News Translation® (Today's English Version, Second Edition) Copyright © 1992 American Bible Society. All rights reserved.

KJV ~ King James Version,1909, public domain

MSG ~ Scripture taken from *The Message*. Copyright © 1993, 1994, 1995, 1996, 2000, 2001, 2002. Used by permission of NavPress Publishing Group.

NAB ~ New American Bible, 2010, 1991, 1986, 1970 Confraternity of Christian Doctrine, Washington, D.C. and are used by permission of the copyright owner. All Rights Reserved.

NOTES: [1] For consistency and clarity, names and pronouns of God have been capitalized throughout including in Bible versions which do not follow that practice. [2] The author capitalizes three other words: "Word" when speaking of God's Word; "Church" when speaking of the Church universal; and "Cross" when referring to the Cross of Calvary. [3] *Italicized* words and [bracketed words] in Scripture and other quotations have been added by the author. [4] The author does not abbreviate the names of Bible books since abbreviations can be unknown to some readers. [5] The author chooses to use a lot of Scripture quotations based on his belief that the Word of God and the Spirit of God are the two dominant factors in changing lives and growing the lives of Christians.

We hope you enjoy this book. Robert Lloyd Russell's goal is to provide high-quality, thought-provoking books that connect truth to real life needs and challenges. For more information on his other books based on Biblical interpretation and application, please visit his author's website BOOKSrlr.

If you find value in this book, please consider writing an online review. The author would be grateful.

In those days there was no king in Israel. Everyone did what was right in his own eyes.

Judges 17:6, 18:1, 19:1, 21:25

Examples of Reader Responses

The writings of Robert Lloyd Russell have received a warm reception by a wide variety of people as seen in the quotes below. His books have received 11 national and international literary awards.

"He writes clearly so that the material is easily understood by both clergy and laity... Very edifying to read." *~ William J. Petersen, Emeritus Senior Acquisitions Editor for Baker Book House and Fleming H. Revell.*

"I loved the book... It is very well written and very understandable." *~ Bob G., inmate*

"I find it most inspirational... You make the reader think, and that is a great talent." *~ Evelyn Cox, homemaker*

"First there was Tozer with *"The Knowledge of the Holy,"* and then Packer gave us *"Knowing God,"* and now Russell has taken us further." *~ Dr. Earl D. Radmacher, General Editor, Nelson Study Bible/New King James Study Bible* [regarding *"GOD'S NATURE: Sonlight Sunlight"*]

"The definitive work on Psalm 1:3. Mr. Russell has a tremendous gift for analogy. The most impressive thing is the way he has built off of existing undeniable Scriptural concepts. I am very impressed with his use of certain Scriptures, such as with regard to trees being deceptive in appearance... His work is very interesting, very clear, and intensely practical." *~ Ronald B. Allen, Senior Professor of Bible Exposition, Dallas Theological Seminary* [regarding *"GOD'S CHILD: Like a Tree"*]

"In summary, this book provides great insight into the thinking of Jim Elliot and also provides a lot of quotable material. I cannot recommend this book highly enough for anyone who is interested in a more fulfilling Christian life. In my opinion, it should be on the reading list of any Christian who seeks a closer relationship with Jesus Christ—especially those in junior high through age 40. It will positively impact their lives!" ~ *Christian Book Club*

"It is must reading." ~ *Richard C. Halverson, Chaplain, U.S. Senate*

"He obviously is hitting on all twelve cylinders! What an exciting insight into Christ as the light of the world. Thank God for people like this who have the background to illuminate some of these Biblical concepts." ~ *Dr. Joe Aldrich, past President, Multnomah Bible College & Biblical Seminary*

"This is so rich! ... This is great! ... Wonderful! ... Mind boggling to say the least! ... Great material for discussion! ... Application pieces are truly inspired!" ~ *Elizabeth Hightower, Women's Ministries Leader, Laurelwood Baptist Church*

"*God's Nature: Sonlight Sunlight* by Robert Lloyd Russell is destined to become a classic in contemporary studies on the character of God." ~ *Richard R. Blake, Seattle Post-Intelligencer*

To

All Members of

The Gideons International

Continuously

Giving God's Word

to Others

FOUNDATIONS

9

1

The Back Story – Judges 17:6

In those days there was no king in Israel. Everyone did what was right in his own eyes.

Judges 17:6, 18:1, 19:1, 21:25

Many a young child in Sunday School has considered the story of Gideon a favorite. As adults we can learn many applicable lessons from Gideon's love and interactions with God and with his Israelite brethren.

Background

In the Bible the Book of Judges comes right after the Book of Joshua. Despite Israel's continuing unfaithfulness, God now provides a series of deliverers in the form of judges. The period of time is the late Bronze Age. It is a story about God and His dealings with His people including both His love and His discipline. God is able and does accomplish His purposes even when His people demonstrate their weakness.

We see a continuing downward cycle of Israel deserting God. Each time Israel receives just consequences, they cry out to God for help (i.e., Judges 3:9, 15; 4:3; 6:6; 10:10).

It is important to note that God was not responding to Israel in justice but in mercy. Israel in no way merits or earns the help of God. Nor does

God step in solely because of Israel's repentance. Rather, God keeps His promises to Israel including that He would give the land of Canaan to them.

Throughout the Book of Judges, we find a repeated pattern of Israel grieving God. Yet in each cycle of their disobedience, God shows compassion for His people and raises up a new leader in the form of a judge for them (i.e., 2:16, 18).

This historical account is really more about God than it is about Gideon.

400 Years

Three times in Scripture we find significant time periods of approximately 400 years:

1. Israel's captivity in Egypt
2. The time of the Judges
3. The time between the Old and New Testaments, known as *The Silent Years*

The Book of Judges

The author of the book of Judges is not known with certainty, but many scholars suspect it was Samuel.

This historical account is believed to be approximately 1425-1050 BC, although there is some disagreement about the time period. Four times we read, "In those days there was no king in Israel. Everyone did what was right in his own eyes" (17:6, 18:1, 19:1, 21:25).

The Book of Judges takes its title from the twelve men and one woman (Deborah) who served as judges during the period leading up to Joshua's death and the time of Samuel. Samuel was the last of the judges and the first of the prophets.

In essence, the book is a summary account of Israel's leaders who came after Joshua and before the first king—Saul (see the book of 1 Samuel).

Judges describes repeated downward cycles by the nation of Israel. Israel was a nation of covenant-breakers. Each time they broke their covenant with God their *Apostasy* eventually led to *Repentance* and then to *Renewal,* or more simply stated *Decline* led to *Defeat* and finally to *Deliverance.*[1]

This cycle of apostasy, then oppression, and finally deliverance by a judge was repeated many times. The book of Judges contains the accounts of the acts of these judges (national heroes).

During the apostasies Israel did not typically completely forsake God. They retained a sense that God was their national God. In a similar way today, the United States considers itself a Christian nation.

One key theme of Judges is that when you put your trust in and dependence on the Lord, He will give you renewed purpose and direction. The judge Gideon emerges as one of the leaders who saved the Israelites from their current enemies.

The Judges

God allowed oppressors to the Israelites – which *tested* them and typically brought about national repentance. The Judges of Israel were God-sent inspired men and a woman who served during periods of oppression, leading the fight against their enemies and gaining back some of their Promised Land. The judges served until the first king of Israel was anointed.

"Now these are the nations that the Lord left, *to test Israel* by them, that is, all in Israel who had not experienced all the wars in Canaan. It was only in order that the generations of the people of Israel might know war, and to teach war to those who had not known it before" (Judges 3:1-2).

The majority of the judges were warriors empowered by the Spirit of God to bring military deliverance to Israel. They each continued until their death.

Basics About Gideon

Gideon served as the fifth judge of Israel and is widely considered Israel's greatest judge. He served from 1145 to 1105 BC. His account is found in Judges 6-8. It occurs at a time when the Israelites were being threatened primarily by the Midianites. This follows the 40 years of peace when judge Deborah spoke of God's prophecies to the nation.

The Midianites were wandering nomads who, with help from the Amalekites and others, would make regular terrorist attacks on Israel. The oppression of Israel by the Midianites for seven years was a direct result of Israel's disobedience to God.

"The people of *Israel did what was evil in the sight of the Lord, and the Lord gave them into the hand of Midian* seven years. And the hand of Midian overpowered Israel, and because of Midian the people of Israel made for themselves dens in the mountains and the caves and the strongholds. For whenever the Israelites planted crops, the Midianites and the Amalekites and the people of the East would come up against them" (Judges 6:1-3).

"And Gideon said to him, 'Please, sir, *if the Lord is with us, why then has all this happened to us?* And where are all His wonderful deeds that our fathers recounted to us, saying, "Did not the Lord bring us up from Egypt?" But now the Lord has forsaken us and given us into the hand of Midian'" (Judges 6:13).

The issue was the Israelites had come to believe in the local fertility gods such as Baal, Ashtoreth, and other male and female deities that were worshipped in nearby nations.

Since His people had once again turned away from God, He allowed the Midianites to abuse the Nation of Israel for seven years by terrorizing them, their livestock, and their land.

I believe Gideon's significance is often under-appreciated. He was a major factor for good as he stepped forward, albeit reluctantly, coming to the aid of Israel. His life story provides many practical lessons for us today.

In fact, Gideon's faithfulness is included in the Hall of Faith chapter in the New Testament. "And what more shall I say? For time would fail me to tell of *Gideon*, Barak, Samson, Jephthah, of David and Samuel and the prophets—who through faith conquered kingdoms, enforced justice, obtained promises" (Hebrews 11:32-33a).

As we read the Old Testament, we realize that the Israelites had to relearn past lessons again and again. They suffered through cycles of disobedience followed by restoration through the obedience and efforts of a judge.

When they were in the sin part of their cycles, they worshipped idols and false gods, while their enemies committed crimes such as stealing their animals and food, and even taxing them. As oppression continued, they would turn back to the One true God.

Sometimes Israel would not entirely wipe out their enemies, leaving remnants of enemy gangs to once again harass them.

The history of Gideon is about God performing miracles by reversing the national tragedy they managed to put themselves in. A key part of this story is how God inspired a timid reluctant young man named Gideon, who stepped up to the plate as his faith emerged. He gained courage and became a decisive spiritual leader. We see in his life many principles to help guide us today.

"Gideon eased into manhood. At best he was an excuse-maker; at worst he was a coward. Until God turned him into a hero... God desired a champion, a man who could rally the nation. Gideon was His man. But first, Gideon had to be coaxed out of hiding... Even after his calling, Gideon continued for a while to make excuses and question whether God had picked the right man. But God kept right on calling him, and training him, and using him. And somewhere, in the midst *of doing,* Gideon became courageous."[2]

Archaeological Confirmation

Gideon is a historical figure. A pottery vessel has been found near Tel Aviv in an area of an ancient settlement, which has inscribed on its handle *Jerubbaal* which is another name for Gideon (6:32, 8:35). The Smithsonian has written about it.[3]

Summary of the Book of Judges

A good summary of the Book of Judges is: "*In those days there was no king in Israel. Everyone did what was right in his own eyes*" (Judges 17:6, 18:1, 19:1, 21:25).

THINK AND GROW

~1~ We learn from Gideon that God does honor faith.

~2~ We learn from Gideon that God does keep His people, even when they stray.

~3~ Do you see any parallels in the nations of the world, including the USA regarding the pattern of spiritual decline? The suggested extra study below might be helpful.

~ *Suggested Extra Study* ~

J. Vernon McGee has made the following observations from the Book of Isaiah:

Isaiah outlines three steps that cause the downfall of nations: (1) spiritual apostasy; (2) moral awfulness; and (3) political anarchy, which is the final stage of any nation. These steps have destroyed nations down through history.

Results of the Era of Judges (Confusion) — Chapters 17-21

    A. Religious Apostasy (The Temple) — Chapters 17-18
    B. Moral Awfulness (The Home) — Chapter 19
    C. Political Anarchy (The State) — Chapters 20-21

~ *Note* ~

The next chapter contains a variety of ways of viewing Israel's cycles of apostasy.

2
Apostasy – 6:1-6

The people of Israel did what was evil in the sight of the Lord, and the Lord gave them into the hand of Midian seven years. And the hand of Midian overpowered Israel, and because of Midian the people of Israel made for themselves the dens that are in the mountains and the caves and the strongholds. For whenever the Israelites planted crops, the Midianites and the Amalekites and the people of the East would come up against them. They would encamp against them and devour the produce of the land, as far as Gaza, and leave no sustenance in Israel and no sheep or ox or donkey. For they would come up with their livestock and their tents; they would come like locusts in number—both they and their camels could not be counted—so that they laid waste the land as they came in. And Israel was brought very low because of Midian. And *the people of Israel cried out for help to the Lord.*

Judges 6:1-6

Leading up to the Book of Judges the twelve tribes of Israel were assigned territories in Canaan. They maintained a commonality in that there was a high priest in charge at a center for national worship in Shiloh.

What was lacking was a central government ruled by a single leader. Each of the tribes was responsible to rule itself. Lacking a combined coordination, each tribe was vulnerable to aggressive nations. Gideon belonged to the tribe of Manasseh.

The Book of Judges is a historical account of multiple times that the Israelites wandered away from God, partly because Israel consisted of a loosely bound together confederation of the twelve tribes.

Various judges from the different tribes met the challenges from opposing and attacking neighbors. Our typical image of the role of a judge is that of settling civilian disputes. In the Book of Judges they were typically leaders empowered with the Spirit of God who brought military deliverance to Israel. They generally maintained this warrior role until their death. (Deborah and Samuel were both primarily involved in settling disputes as opposed to being deliverers.)

Apostasy

Apostasy consisted of rejection of spiritual truths – whether in the mind or in actions. It included both unconsciously abandoning the truth and of course deliberate actions such as rebellion, abandonment, or defection.

The apostasy in the Book of Judges was not a complete forsaking of God, but a subtle forsaking. The people maintained a sense of God being their national God Who had been historically faithful to them.

The problem was that they started to also believe in some of the fertility gods which were being worshipped by cultures throughout the region – gods such as Baal and Ashtoreth. In essence, they were doing exactly what Joshua had previously warned then against:

"Now therefore *fear the Lord and serve him in sincerity and in faithfulness.* Put away the gods that your fathers served beyond the River and in Egypt, and serve the Lord. And if it is evil in your eyes to serve the Lord, *choose this day whom you will serve,* whether the gods your fathers served in the region beyond the River, or the gods of the

Amorites in whose land you dwell. But *as for me and my house, we will serve the Lord.* Then the people answered, 'Far be it from us that we should forsake the Lord to serve other gods'" (Joshua 24:14-16).

We find the record of Joshua's death early in the Book of Judges. Unfortunately, the Israelites soon did exactly what Joshua warned against!

"When Joshua dismissed the people, the people of Israel went each to his inheritance to take possession of the land. And *the people served the Lord all the days of Joshua,* and all the days of the elders who outlived Joshua, who had seen all the great work that the Lord had done for Israel. And *Joshua the son of Nun, the servant of the Lord, died at the age of 110 years.* And they buried him within the boundaries of his inheritance in Timnath-heres, in the hill country of Ephraim, north of the mountain of Gaash. And all that generation also were gathered to their fathers. And *there arose another generation after them who did not know the Lord* or the work that he had done for Israel" (Judges 2:6-10)

Quick Change

Continuing the passage immediately above we read:

"And *the people of Israel did what was evil in the sight of the Lord and served the Baals.* And they abandoned the Lord, the God of their fathers, who had brought them out of the land of Egypt. *They went after other gods,* from among the gods of the peoples who were around them, and bowed down to them. And *they provoked the Lord to anger.* They abandoned the Lord and served the Baals and the Ashtaroth. So *the anger of the Lord was kindled against Israel,* and He gave them over to plunderers, who plundered them. And He sold them into the hand of their surrounding enemies, so that they could no longer withstand their enemies. Whenever they marched out, the hand of the Lord was against them for harm, as the Lord had warned, and as the Lord had sworn to them. And they were in terrible distress" (Judges 2:11-15).

We see a clear pattern emerge as the passage continues.

"Then *the Lord raised up judges*, who saved them out of the hand of those who plundered them. Yet *they did not listen to their judges*, for they whored after other gods and bowed down to them. *They soon turned aside* from the way in which their fathers had walked, who had obeyed the commandments of the Lord, and they did not do so. *Whenever the Lord raised up judges for them, the Lord was with the judge*, and He saved them from the hand of their enemies all the days of the judge. For the Lord was moved to pity by their groaning because of those who afflicted and oppressed them. But *whenever the judge died, they turned back and were more corrupt than their fathers*, going after other gods, serving them and bowing down to them. They did not drop any of their practices or their stubborn ways" (Judges 2:16-20).

Cycles In Judges

In the Book of Judges there are cycles of apostasy which typically follow this pattern:

1. *Freedom*
2. Apostasy
3. Bondage
4. Humility and Dependence
5. Deliverance
6. *Freedom*

There have been other descriptions of the apostasy cycles in the Book of Judges, most of which typically have no source attached to them. Here are some examples:

God sent judges to Israel who repeatedly followed *a fourfold cycle*:

1. *Apostasy*: the Israelites doing what is evil in the sight of the Lord

2. *Servitude*: God allows the nation to be conquered and oppressed by a neighboring nation

3. *Supplication*: the people cry out to God

4. *Salvation*: God sends a Judge to deliver the Israelites

The cycle then repeats after the Judge dies.

1. *Peace in the land – Israel serves the Lord*
2. Israel does evil in the eyes of the Lord
3. God punishes Israel by enslavement
4. Israel asks God for help
5. God raises up a Judge
6. Israel is delivered
7. *Peace in the land – Israel serves the Lord*

1. *Israel does good*
2. Israel does bad
3. Israel gets punished
4. Israel asks for God's help
5. God sends them a Judge
6. Israel is saved
7. *Israel does good*

1. *Peace under a Judge*
2. The people turn from God
3. God judges by delivering them to their enemies
4. Israel turns back to God
5. God sends a Judge to rescue the people
6. *Peace under a Judge*

1. *Israel serves the Lord*
2. Israel falls into sin and idolatry
3. Israel is enslaved
4. Israel cries out to the Lord
5. God raises up a Judge
6. Israel is delivered
7. *Israel serves the Lord*

The Tytler Cycle of History

1. *Bondage*
2. Spiritual Faith
3. Courage
4. Liberty
5. Abundance
6. Selfishness
7. Complacency
8. Apathy
9. Dependence
10. *Bondage*

The Cycles of Apostasy

1. *Rest*
2. Relapse
3. Ruin

4. Repentance
5. Restoration
6. *Rest*

Specific Cycles

Consider the cycles of *"Sin—Servitude—Supplication—Salvation"* in the Book of Judges.

Some scholars list Eight Cycles of Apostasy in the Book of Judges followed by Restoration.

#	Judge	Reference	Oppressor	Length	Result
1	Othniel	3:7-11	Mesopotamia	8 years	40 years of peace
2	Ehud	3:12-30	Ammonites, Amalekites	18 years	80 years of peace
3	Shamgar	3:31	Philistines		
4	Deborah & Barak	4:1-5:31	Canaanites	20 years	40 years of peace
5	Gideon	6:1-8:35	Midianites	7 years	40 years of peace
6	*Abimelech**, Tola, Jair	9:1-10:5	Ammonites		
7	Jephthah	10-6-12:15	Philistines, Ammonites	6 years	
8	Samson	13:1-16:31	Philistines	40 years	

** Not a judge*

These cycles of falling away, oppression, and finally deliverance by a judge occurred over about two centuries. The root issue was idolatry – being double-minded with allegiance to more than the One True God.

Fifth Apostasy

Gideon ruled during a time of sin leading to oppression and later deliverance. He is somewhat different than the other judges in that the Scriptures record more detail about his activities – in today's vernacular we would say that Gideon received "a lot of press."

THINK AND GROW

~1~ It is so easy to let down our spiritual guard and fall away from constant fellowship with God.

~2~ God is patient and merciful – always eager for restored fellowship with us.

~3~ I have come to the conclusion that today many Christians are a lot like the Israelites. When things are going well, we have a tendency to rely on ourselves and give ourselves some of the glory. Often it isn't until we are in our lowest moments that we turn to God. I sum it up this way:

The Cycle of Sin in Some Established Christian Lives

1. *Worship and obedience to God*
2. A spiritually productive period
3. Becoming knowledgeable and proud
4. Focused on stuff
5. Controlled by repetitive sin
6. Crying out to God
7. God gives freedom once again
8. *Worship and obedience to God*

~ Related to #1 & #2 ~ "Worship and obedience to God" & "A spiritually productive period"

Following conversion, it is very common to have a "honeymoon period" of great love and appreciation for the Savior.

~ Related to #3 ~ "Becoming knowledgeable and proud"

I believe that of all forms of pride God must view spiritual pride as the worst.

"Now these things, brethren, I have figuratively transferred to myself and Apollos for your sakes, *that you may learn in us not to think beyond what is written, that none of you may be puffed up on behalf of one against the other.* For who makes you differ from another? And *what do you have that you did not receive? Now if you did indeed receive it, why do you boast as if you had not received it?"* (1 Corinthians 4:6-7 nkjv).

~ Related to #4 ~ "Focused on stuff"

Worship of idols in our day is very subtle. Anything that becomes as important as or more important than your Savior is an idol. An activity can be good intrinsically, but when it supersedes your love and devotion for your Savior, it becomes an idol.

An idol is an issue of our affections – it can quickly lead to self-centeredness, love of possessions, position, power. It can even be a worthwhile hobby, sport, or activity. It is sometimes closely connected to greed and pride.

~ Anecdote ~

There was a time when I had the opportunity to fulfill one of my boyhood dreams – to build my own HO model railroad. I took to it in grand fashion. I had all the track laid, four locomotives with choices of many railroad cars. It had a complex (for its day) control system where each of our four family members could run their train independently at the same time on the same tracks. It also had a small town with an independently-run trolley. Next on my agenda was the landscaping.

There was nothing wrong with my hobby except I began to realize I was so occupied with this activity that I no longer had much time for spiritual matters in my life. After much prayer and thought, I sold the whole setup and returned to a more God-focused life.

"*No one can serve two masters*, for either he will hate the one and love the other, or he will be devoted to the one and despise the other. *You cannot serve God and money*" (Matthew 6:24).

"Draw near to God, and He will draw near to you. Cleanse your hands, you sinners, and *purify your hearts, you double-minded*. Be wretched and mourn and weep. Let your laughter be turned to mourning and your joy to gloom. *Humble yourselves before the Lord*, and He will exalt you" (James 4:8-10).

"For many, of whom I have often told you and now tell you even with tears, walk as enemies of the Cross of Christ. Their end is destruction, their god is their belly, and they glory in their shame, with minds set on earthly things. But our citizenship is in heaven, and from it we await a Savior, the Lord Jesus Christ, who will transform our lowly body to be like his glorious body, by the power that enables him even to subject all things to Himself" (Philippians 3:18-21).

~ Related to #5 & #6 ~ "Controlled by repetitive sin" & "Crying out to God"

Early in my Christian life I became distressed because I kept finding myself crying out to God for help each time I got myself into a difficult position – it made me feel guilty. While it is true we should remain in constant communion with God, I found comfort in Scripture and especially in the Psalms where I found many examples of God's people crying out to God in times of significant stress. Consider one example:

"*In my distress I called upon the Lord; to my God I called*. From His temple He heard my voice,

and my cry came to His ears" (2 Samuel 22:7, see also Psalm 18:6).

The danger of not crying out to God in time of trouble is that Satan often uses our troubles to cause us to begin doubting our salvation. Stay close to God!

~ Related to #7 & #8 ~ "God gives freedom once again" & "Worship and obedience to God"

God answers your call and restores you to faith and fruitfulness.

~ Comment ~

If you are a Christian, then just like each of the judges, God has specific tasks for you to do.

~ Editor's Note ~

If you are unsure of what God has in mind for you, I recommend another book: "*GOD'S DESIRE: How To Please God,*" eBook ISBN: 978-1393211785, ASIN: B08H4F619W; or print edition: ISBN: 979-8223962915, approximately 200 pages.

This book starts with the complex subject of the will of God presented in an innovative, easy-to-understand, and quick-read format that concisely explains the three main components of God's will. This is critical to understanding how to please God.

The illustrated "*Christian Life Model*" and "*Christian Guidance Model*" graphically display what God desires from His children and how they can be assured of making correct decisions throughout their lives. The book closes with a concise description of the benefits of following the two models.

~4~ How about your current life?

~~~a~ We need the Spirit of God to help us identify any misplaced priorities in our lives.
~~~

~~~b~ Are there any idols in your life?

~~~c~ Are changes in your current lifestyle needed?

3

A Prophet – 6:6-10

And Israel was brought very low because of Midian. And the people of Israel cried out for help to the Lord. When the people of Israel cried out to the Lord on account of the Midianites, *the Lord sent a prophet to the people of Israel*. And he said to them, "Thus says the Lord, the God of Israel: I led you up from Egypt and brought you out of the house of slavery. And I delivered you from the hand of the Egyptians and from the hand of all who oppressed you, and drove them out before you and gave you their land. And I said to you, 'I am the Lord your God; you shall not fear the gods of the Amorites in whose land you dwell.' But you have not obeyed My voice."

Judges 6:6-10

40-Year Bookends

The Israelites had done evil and the Lord delivered them from twenty years of oppression by the Canaanites. Then they experienced 40 years of rest (Judges 5:31). But they fell right back into idolatry and were oppressed by the Midianites for seven years. This is the point where Gideon appears, and following his time as Judge they will experience another 40 years of peace (Judges 8:28).

Israel Cries Out

Once again, the Israelites had turned to worshipping other gods and idols. God then allowed Israel's enemies to be used as instruments in the chastening of His people.

The Midianites oppressed Israel for years. When a nation is under constant siege everybody is affected. The Israelites were hiding in caves and fortified locations.

The Midianites were "highly mobile Bedouin marauders mounted on camels. They infiltrated from the desert and filled the valleys with their flocks and tents, harassing the Israelites populace scattered in open settlements."[4]

Eventually the Israelites cried out to God for help. This time a small weak lad named Gideon, who was busy threshing wheat, will become God's instrument of deliverance.

God Responds

A prophet in the Bible is a person who has been inspired by God to deliver a divine message to a person or persons.

"The Lord sent a prophet to the people of Israel." Who was this unnamed prophet? The Bible does not tell us. There have been a number of speculations including Samuel, Phineas, and others. Keep in mind that this prophet was an *unnamed* messenger from God. The most important thing to realize is that God hears our prayers and He responds:

"When the people of Israel cried out to the Lord on account of the Midianites, *the Lord sent a prophet to the people of Israel*" (Judges 6:7-8a).

The key thing is that when God's people sincerely turn back to Him, He responds with loving mercy and grace. In the cycles of apostasy in the Book of Judges, God responds each time by sending a deliverer.

Gideon Overview

Before we get into the heart of Gideon's story, here is a quick overview:

Speaking through one of His prophets, God reminds His people: "Thus says the Lord, the God of Israel: I led you up from Egypt and brought you out of the house of slavery" (Judges 6:8b). God knew His people had poor memories of past blessing and needed to be reminded of His past goodness to them as they headed into their next apostasy crisis.

Those who remembered God's past faithfulness, mercy, love, and power were able to handle new difficult times much better. God will soon help them during the difficult times ahead by utilizing a reluctant Judge named Gideon.

God also reminded them, "you have not obeyed my voice" (Judges 6:10b). God was in essence telling them that the root cause of their current problems was not the oppressor Midianites but their own disobedience. You, Israel, have brought this on yourselves. The human tendency to blame others, which started with Adam in the Garden of Eden, was clearly in their minds. The fact they were crying out to God indicates they did not recognize their own guilt and need for repentance.

THINK AND GROW

~1 ~ God often uses tough times in the lives of His people to get their attention and bring them back into close communion with Him.

~~~a~ God was displeased with the Israelites, but He still listened and responded to their cries.

~~~b~ Have you ever experienced this?

~2~ In this example it is important to see how God uses mercy and great grace to restore His wandering children.

~3~ Do you think the Israelites would have been better or worse off if God had left them alone?

~4~ Have you ever blamed an outside source for a problem of your own making?

4
An Angel – 6:11-12

Now the *angel of the Lord came and sat under the terebinth at Ophrah,* which belonged to Joash the Abiezrite, while his son Gideon was beating out wheat in the winepress to hide it from the Midianites. And the *angel of the Lord appeared to him* and said to him, "The Lord is with you, O mighty man of valor."

Judges 6:11-12

Angel Appearance

In this remarkable passage we find the record of "the angel of the Lord" appearing to Gideon. Perhaps more interesting is that the angel appeared as an ordinary man.

One would expect an appearance of an angel to be some grandiose event. Another somewhat normal expectation is that the appearance of an angel would be to an important person – at least important from a spiritual reputation point of view.

In this case the Lord was looking for the least likely warrior for the job He needed to be done. God needed a humble man who would give God the credit for any victory.

"Consider your calling, brothers: not many of you were wise according to worldly standards, not many were powerful, not many were of noble birth. But God chose what is foolish in the world to shame the wise; *God chose what is weak in the world to shame the strong;* God chose what is low and despised in the world, even things that are not, to bring to nothing things that are, *so that no human being might boast in the presence of God*" (1 Corinthians 1:26-29).

When God chooses someone for a job, He will be with that person until the end. In this case God chose a very ordinary man named Gideon – about whom the Book of Judges records more than any other judge.

A Message

In an act of compassion for His people, God sends the "angel of the Lord" to Gideon.

The angel is sitting under an oak tree as Gideon is going about his life. As if that isn't surprising enough, the angel announces to Gideon: "The Lord is with you, O mighty man of valor."

What me? You've got the wrong man! "Man of valor"? Why, I haven't even served in the military, you must have come to the wrong man!

Gideon might have even surmised that he was being mocked. He knew he was anything but a warrior kind of man. But Gideon did not realize that the angel was really foretelling his future as a man of valor. Gideon was receiving a commission from God to deliver Israel from the oppression of the Midianites.

Gideon was unable to believe what was happening. He knew he was weak – anything but strong. He came from a family that was no longer worshipping God, but rather false gods. Gideon thought he was not good enough to be used by God.

But God, through His angel, was telling Gideon to focus on Him rather than on himself. Gideon should rely on God's strength rather than his situation and his own weakness.

It is a matter of correct focus.

"At the end of that time, *I, Nebuchadnezzar, raised my eyes toward heaven, and my sanity was restored... At the same time that my sanity was restored, my honor and splendor were returned to me...* Now I, Nebuchadnezzar, praise and exalt and glorify the King of heaven, because everything He does is right and all His ways are just. And those who walk in pride He is able to humble" (Daniel 4:34a, 36a, 37 niv).

The message from the angel was really clear – Gideon needed to accept it.

A Reaction

I suspect Gideon didn't believe the angel. He already had a busy life working his family's farm. But our behavior is not necessarily indicative of our identity as a child of God.

Do you think that this whole episode with an angel might have made Gideon wonder if he was going to die after having this incredible divine experience?

Whatever his thoughts Gideon was hesitant to trust in what the angel was saying. What the angel was telling him just did not make much sense to him: "The Lord is with you, O mighty man of valor."

We will look more at Gideon's response in a later chapter.

A Theophany

What is a theophany? The word comes from two Greek words, "God" and "appearance." So theophany is a word for an appearance of God – an actual appearance to man which expresses the presence and character of God. Theophanies are recorded throughout the Old Testament.

So when the Angel of the Lord appeared to Gideon, *we recognize this is as a theophany* – an Old Testament appearance of Jesus Christ, in human, bodily form, but before His incarnation in Bethlehem. When it is Jesus who appears as opposed to God the Father, it is sometimes called a *Christophany*.

Some examples of theophanies in the Old Testament include:

- Abraham sacrificing Isaac – Genesis 22:15-16
- Moses and the burning bush – Exodus 3:2, 6
- An angel speaking to Israel – Judges 2:1
- An angel speaking to Gideon – Judges 6:12

The essence of a theophany is the reality of God's presence. There are at least sixteen examples in the Old Testament of the angel of the Lord making an appearance.

It is interesting to note that unlike Isaiah, Ezekiel, John, and Paul, Gideon did not fall into a traumatic sleep from seeing the glory of God. Quite the opposite, Gideon carried on a conversation with the angel of the Lord.

THINK AND GROW

~1~ What insecurities do you have?

~2~ God sees the potential in every man.

~3~ God calls leaders from unlikely places.

~4~ Have you ever sensed a very strong sense of God's presence?

~~~*~ If so, and in a group, would you be willing to share your experience?

~ *Note* ~

If we think God only speaks through traumatic or grandiose happenings, we will most likely miss out on great intimate and productive moments with and for Him.

"I do not cease to give thanks for you, remembering you in my prayers, that the God of our Lord Jesus Christ, *the Father of glory, may give you a spirit of wisdom and of revelation in the knowledge of Him, having the eyes of your hearts enlightened*, that you may know what is the hope to which He has called you, what are the riches of His glorious inheritance in the saints, and what is *the immeasurable greatness of His power toward us who believe*, according to the working of His great might that He worked in Christ when He raised Him from the dead and seated Him at His right hand in the heavenly places" (Ephesians 1:16-20).

~5~ Have you ever felt God was speaking to you specifically?

~~~a~ If His voice fell on unresponsive ears, how do you feel about it now?

~~~b~ If you responded positively, what were the results?
~~~

5
A Man – 6:11-14

Now the angel of the Lord came and sat under the terebinth at Ophrah, which belonged to Joash the Abiezrite, while his son *Gideon was beating out wheat in the winepress to hide it from the Midianites.* And the angel of the Lord appeared to him and said to him, "The Lord is with you, O mighty man of valor." And Gideon said to him, "Please, my lord, if the Lord is with us, why then has all this happened to us? And where are all His wonderful deeds that our fathers recounted to us, saying, 'Did not the Lord bring us up from Egypt?' But now the Lord has forsaken us and given us into the hand of Midian." And the Lord turned to him and said, "Go in this might of yours and save Israel from the hand of Midian; do not I send you?"

Judges 6:11-14

Gideon's Name

Gideon's name is mentioned at least forty times in the Book of Judges.[5]

His name has a Hebrew origin that has a root meaning of "feller,"[6] or "hewer."[7]

The root meaning has seen a variety of expressions: "one who cuts down," "one who cuts to pieces," "cutter of trees," or "feller of trees." One commentator says "he wielded his axe with reckless abandonment until all the trees lay horizontally."

Some claim his name means: "overcomer," "great warrior," "great destroyer," "mighty warrior," or "strong man," but I am not sure how they arrive at those meanings.

Gideon Overview

Gideon's hometown was Ophrah in the Valley of Jezreel. His father was Joash from the tribe[1] of Manasseh (who was of the family of Abiezer). Gideon's family worked the family's farm. He was the youngest in a poor family. He was a weak man from a meek family.

The family and the other Israelites lived in constant fear because neighboring groups would steal their grain and livestock. The Israelite people had to seek out shelter in caves to protect themselves and what little food they had.

Gideon came from a humble clan and was considered the least likely to succeed in his family. But God saw him differently. God saw Gideon as he would become in the strength of the Lord, and that is the way He sees you and me.

He came from a family that did not obey God and had drifted into worshipping false gods.

It was his father Joash and others like him who were responsible for Israel's oppression by the Midianites. Unfortunately, it is not clear from Scripture whether Joash or any other family members ever returned to worshiping the One True God – however, quite possibly they did (see Judges 8:27b).

When we meet Gideon in Scripture, he is busy threshing wheat in a winepress. This was not the typical thing to do but was done to protect

---

1. https://www.learnreligions.com/12-tribes-of-israel-700165

the grain from invading enemies. Gideon was working in hiding down in the winepress so that the Midianites would not steal from him. Gideon was threshing grain with his threshing stick in a way that when it hit the wheat the grain seeds came loose from the straw. The grain would be used to make bread. While he was working, the angel of the Lord came and sat down under an oak tree near him.

In summary, when we meet Gideon he is an average Israelite who is fearful of their terrorist nomadic enemies – primarily the Amorites, but also other nations. His life was full of trouble.

Like us, Gideon did not understand the divine discipline God was bringing upon the nation of Israel: "The angel of the Lord appeared to him and said to him, 'The Lord is with you, O mighty man of valor.' and Gideon said to him, 'Please, my lord, if the Lord is with us, *why then has all this happened to us?"* (Judges 6:12-13a).

Later, as a result of God's call he became a Judge and military commander, an honored man in Israel. He judged Israel for forty years. He fathered Abimelech as well as seventy unnamed sons.

THINK AND GROW

~1~ God often uses tough times to get our attention.

~2~ Looking back on your life, do you think God has ever spoken to you and you failed to respond?

~3~ Do you believe God could do great things through you?

~~~a~ Do you believe that God desires to use you in His kingdom work?
~~~

~~~b~ Are you open to and willing to follow His directions for your life?

~ Editor's Note ~

If you are having trouble knowing God's specific direction for your life, you might want to consider the book: *"GOD'S DESIRE FOR YOU: How To Please God,"* eBook ISBN: 978-1393211785, ASIN: B08H4F619W; or print edition ISBN: 979-8223962915, approximately 200 pages.
~~~

6

A Winepress – 6:11-14

Now the angel of the Lord came and sat under the terebinth at Ophrah, which belonged to Joash the Abiezrite, while his son *Gideon was beating out wheat in the winepress to hide it from the Midianites.* And the angel of the Lord appeared to him and said to him, "The Lord is with you, O mighty man of valor." And Gideon said to him, "Please, my lord, if the Lord is with us, why then has all this happened to us? And where are all His wonderful deeds that our fathers recounted to us, saying, 'Did not the Lord bring us up from Egypt?' But now the Lord has forsaken us and given us into the hand of Midian." And the Lord turned to him and said, "Go in this might of yours and save Israel from the hand of Midian; do not I send you?"

Judges 6:11-14

Gideon was totally unaware of it, but God had chosen him to deliver Israel from the oppression of the Midianites (descendants of Abraham and Keturah). The historical account begins during the wheat harvest and Gideon was in hiding threshing wheat in a winepress in fear of the Midianites.

The Setting

The children of Israel were living in dens, caves, and other strongholds: the oppression of the Midianites which was a result of the sin of Israel brought Israel into humiliation. Before they turned back to God they

45

had to be humbled, living as cave-dwellers instead of properly civilized people.

Israel would sow their crops, but when harvest was due the Midianites would come. The Midianites did not occupy the land, but came at the time of harvest to steal what the Israelites had grown. Not only did they steal their crops but also their livestock and other possessions.

As far as Gaza: "That is, the whole breadth of the land, from Jordan to the coast of the Mediterranean Sea. Thus the whole land was ravaged and the inhabitants deprived of the necessaries of life."[8]

Both the Midianites and their camels were without number. They were a desert-dwelling people and they dominated Israel because of their effective use of camels. "It is clear that the use of this angular and imposing beast struck terror in the hearts of the Israelites."[9]

Archaeological Evidence

There have been many "grain pits" found from the period of the Judges. These support the Biblical account of the insecurity of the times.

Humor

This scene opens rather humorously. Gideon is basically in hiding in a winepress at the time an angel of the Lord calls him "a mighty man of valor."

A winepress is not the normal place to be threshing wheat. But Gideon was afraid because of the constant turmoil caused by the Midianites. Normally one would thresh the wheat out in a field – often on hilltops. The chaff would be blown away by the breezes. But because of the constant raids on the crops, animals, and possessions of the Israelites by the desert nomads, Gideon was threshing wheat in a somewhat hidden and unlikely place. The threshing of the wheat in a winepress was a way to keep this job hidden from the oppressors.

The name Midian means "brawling or contentious," an appropriate description of how the Midianites moved from city to city, plain to plain, and people to people stealing all that lay in their path. One writer has described their marauding being like the descending of vast clouds of locusts.

The winepress was "a place of privacy; he could not make a threshing-floor in open day as the custom was, and bring either the wheel over the grain, or tread it out with the feet of the oxen, for fear of the Midianites, who were accustomed to come and take it away as soon as threshed."[10]

Courageous

God had allowed the Midianites to oppress the Israelites for seven long years. Out of fear of the Midianites, Gideon was threshing the wheat in a hidden place.

One could see Gideon as a courageous person in this scene. He was continuing to work while the enemy was likely nearby. Many of his countrymen were hiding in caves or other places. While others were hiding, Gideon was out there working – even if he was threshing in a hidden winepress as opposed to being out in the openness of a field. Gideon was providing grain for bread to help hold off starvation of his family and neighbors.

Doing the threshing in a winepress was a way of trying to do it in secret from the marauding enemies. The threshing of wheat was hard difficult work and also somewhat humiliating (especially being done in secret).

Gideon must have been a terrified young man as he secretly threshes a meager crop of wheat at an ancient wine press. Recall that he is a member of the weakest clan in Israel and he is the youngest in his family. He has never stood up to the Midianites, who dominate Israel. Nothing about him seems destined for greatness – but he was faithful to what needed to be done for his people.

It was during this time of threshing in secret that we see the angel of the Lord speak to him and call him "a mighty man of courage." An interesting comment since Gideon seemed to serve the idol of fear.

THINK AND GROW

Gideon like many of us today trusted in what his finite mind could grasp. As things went wrong, instead of seeking God he tended to blame God. Gideon failed to recognize his people's failure was the cause of the justice and punishment of God.

~1~ Today's tasks, even the most mundane of them, are often preparation for tomorrow's activities.

~2~ Sometimes bad things happen to good people. The causes of circumstances aren't always clear.

Jesus said, "You may be sons of your Father who is in heaven. For He makes His sun rise on the evil and on the good, and sends rain on the just and on the unjust" (Matthew 5:45-46).

~3~ Difficult circumstances are not necessarily the result of our own, or others' sin.

~~~a~ Have you personally known individuals whose life was ruined through alcohol, drugs, gambling, pornography, or other bad choices?

~~~b~ Have you known any "successful" accomplished individuals who essentially lost everything because of sin's dominance in their life?

~4~ Do you have an addiction which might be holding you back from the life God desires for you?

~~~*~ If so, are you willing to deal with it with God's strength?
~~~

7
A Call – 6:13-18

And Gideon said to him, "Please, my lord, if the Lord is with us, why then has all this happened to us? And where are all His wonderful deeds that our fathers recounted to us, saying, 'Did not the Lord bring us up from Egypt?' But now the Lord has forsaken us and given us into the hand of Midian." And *the Lord turned to him and said, "Go in this might of yours and save Israel from the hand of Midian; do not I send you?"* And he said to him, "Please, Lord, how can I save Israel? Behold, my clan is the weakest in Manasseh, and I am the least in my father's house." And the Lord said to him, "But I will be with you, and you shall strike the Midianites as one man." And he said to him, "If now I have found favor in your eyes, then show me a sign that it is you who speak with me. Please do not depart from here until I come to you and bring out my present and set it before you." And he said, "I will stay till you return."

Judges 6:13-18

When God chooses to call someone to a specific task, it is never because of their strengths or abilities. God seeks willingness, commitment, and perhaps most importantly faith, trust, humility, and obedience.

Circumstances are also not a concern to God. True, you need to be in a place where God needs a task performed – or He can move you to the right spot. We should not allow our current circumstances to define our responses to a call from God.

"God is looking for people through whom He can do the impossible – what a pity that we plan only the things that we think we can do by ourselves."[11]

The important thing about a call from God is the two choices we face – to accept the call and please God or refuse the call and miss out on the blessings that are associated with following God's will.

The Scene

When Gideon first saw the angel of the Lord, he had no conception that he was at a major turning point in his life. At that moment the goal of Gideon was to survive another day of making grain for bread without being discovered by the enemies. Gideon had absolutely no idea what plans God had for him as he went about his work.

Gideon was part of a family that had slipped into apostasy and the worship of other gods. God had sent affliction to the Israelites. This affected Gideon so much that he questioned whether God was really on his side. "Please, my lord, *if the Lord is with us, why then has all this happened to us?*" (Judges 6:13).

Gideon failed to recognize that just because circumstances were not good, it did not mean that God had abandoned them. This was in part how God was working in the lives of the Israelites.

God's Call

When God called Gideon, he thought of himself as *insignificant*. This was actually a very good thing since God does not typically work through proud people. Gideon lacked self-confidence but what he needed was more God-confidence.

Likewise, as we go about our daily lives God may interrupt our routines by presenting a specific task for us to do for His kingdom.

Did Gideon at this point realize that God desired to use him to defeat the fearful marauders of Midianites and other surrounding tribes? I don't think so! Did he realize that if he followed God's call his people would no longer have to hide in places like caves – but rather could live out their lives in peace? I don't think so!

Gideon's Reluctance

Gideon actually tried to talk God out of His request by pointing out stuff God already knew about him. Here was his initial reply to God:

"And he said to him, 'Please, Lord, *how can I save Israel? Behold, my clan is the weakest in Manasseh, and I am the least in my father's house'*" (Judges 6:15). It was as if Gideon thought he was telling God something He didn't know. God did of course know about Gideon's insignificance and perhaps chose him largely because of it. In Gideon's initial reluctance he had a tendency to depersonalize God's call with phrases like "my clan" and "least in my father's house."

Gideon probably had many concerns, even opposing fears. For example, what would his father and family think if he left the current gods of his family and went back to faith in God? On the other hand, would he face God's wrath if he refused God's request?

With the benefit of the New Testament, we have learned about the upside-down realities of being a child of God on earth: "But He said to me, 'My grace is sufficient for you, for *My power is made perfect in weakness.*' Therefore I will boast all the more gladly of my weaknesses, so that the power of Christ may rest upon me. For the sake of Christ, then, I am content with weaknesses, insults, hardships, persecutions, and calamities. For *when I am weak, then I am strong*" (2 Corinthians 12:9-10).

God chose Gideon *because* of his weakness – any glory from victory would obviously be due to God rather than to Gideon.

As we read through the Old and New Testaments, many times we find how amazing it is that God typically chooses "weak" people to do amazing things.

To Gideon's Credit

Gideon was troubled by Israel's oppressors, but he was not apathetic or fatalistic about the current situation they found themselves in. "And he [Gideon] said to Him, 'If now I have found favor in Your eyes, then show me a sign that it is You who speaks with me. Please do not depart from here until I come to You and bring out my present and set it before You.' And He said, 'I will stay till you return'" (Judges 6:17-18).

THINK AND GROW

We are similar to Gideon in that we easily forget God's past blessings and where we have come from. If we become focused on outward circumstances, it is easy to begin to blame God or question His love for us.

> *~ Anecdote ~*
>
> Early in my Christian life I began a notebook which I labeled "Significant Events in My Spiritual Life." Periodically looking back and reviewing its contents has

been a great blessing and has strengthened my faith. I highly recommend this practice.

God is still in the business of calling out individuals to do specific work for Him. He chooses individuals to do specific different tasks. What He calls another to do may be different than what He calls you to do.

God sees the potential in each of His children. He knows your true value and abilities. He also has a deep love for each of His children.

God does not ask anyone to do something unless He is committed to be with them in the task He has given. God goes with you.

God chooses weak things to accomplish big things. You and God are able to conquer.

There is an old saying, "God does not call the qualified but rather He qualifies the called."

God sees us differently than how we see ourselves. He works patiently with us and molds us. Our proper response is to be willing to "go in whatever strength we have," taking a single step at a time, as we follow His leading. God will do the rest.

~1~ Have you ever felt like Gideon: If God is real in my life, why has this happened to me?

~2~ In the past what have you done when you faced a difficulty, conflict, or challenge that you felt inadequate to handle?

~3~ Instead of trying to escape your weaknesses, have you learned to see your deficiencies as given to you by God that He might receive glory from your accomplishments done in His name and power?

~4~ As we see with Gideon, God speaks to ordinary people who are going about their routine duties.

~5~ Throughout Scripture we see God using individuals rather than committees.

~6~ Is your faith strong enough to doubt your doubts and believe your beliefs?

8

A Response – 6:16-18

And the Lord said to him, "But I will be with you, and you shall strike the Midianites as one man." And he said to Him, "*If now I have found favor* in Your eyes, then *show me a sign* that it is You who speaks with me. Please do not depart from here until I come to you and bring out my present and set it before You." And He said, "I will stay till you return."

Judges 6:16-18

Have you ever had doubt about spiritual matters? Have you ever been concerned about what God wanted you to do? Have you ever questioned if God can use you? Gideon was not sure of the direction he should go. He had honest sincere doubts.

At times we can be unsure of ourselves or our abilities. We can focus on insufficiencies, our lack of knowledge or equipment. We can feel incompetent or overwhelmed. We sometimes question if it is really God directing us. This was Gideon's situation.

God's Assurance

Gideon was insecure, but we read, "The Lord said to him, 'But *I will be with you*.'"

Intellectually we may believe that God and I are all we need for victory, but in our humanity with all its complex emotions we have trouble believing it enough to act upon the truth.

God has promised to be with His servants throughout history. Take for example Isaac (Genesis 26:3), Jacob (Genesis 31:3), Moses (Deuteronomy 31:23), Joshua (Joshua 1:5, 3:7), Gideon (Judges 6:16), Jeroboam (1 Kings 11:38), and Jacob (Isaiah 43:2).

Perhaps one of the most well-known passages in the Bible is Psalm 23 which includes: "Even though I walk through the valley of the shadow of death, *I will fear no evil, for You are with me*; Your rod and your staff, they comfort me" (Psalm 23:4).

Gideon's Response

Gideon did the typical human thing and resisted what God was asking him to do. Gideon was focused on his inadequacies. He focused on why he couldn't do it instead the fact that He could accomplish it through Him. We see this human trait throughout Scripture when God calls someone (one clear example is Moses in Exodus 3:11).

Focusing on the wrong things will always lead us astray.

"And Gideon said to him, 'Please, sir, *if the Lord is with us, why then has all this happened to us?* And where are all His wonderful deeds that our fathers recounted to us, saying, "Did not the Lord bring us up from Egypt?" But now *the Lord has forsaken us and given us into the hand of Midian*'" (Judges 6:13). Gideon's focus was on current circumstances.

Gideon doubted God's call and was sure that he was not a man of bravery: "Please, Lord, *how can I save Israel*? Behold, *my clan is the weakest* in Manasseh, and *I am the least* in my father's house" (Judges

6:15). It is clear that Gideon lacked faith and confidence in God's ability to work through him. Gideon's focus was on his abilities rather than God's strength.

Gideon was skeptical – how could he serve the Lord effectively? Gideon was seeking proof in the form of a sign from God.

THINK AND GROW

God would love to use you for His kingdom work just as He used Gideon. Each of His children is used in different ways. All are given important tasks to do.

Gideon's experience demonstrates that God uses weak, inadequate, fearful, but humble individuals to do His work on earth.

~1~ What do you think? Did Gideon have a weak faith or was he doing due diligence in trying to verify that it was truly God he was dealing with?

~2~ Do you fight with feelings of inadequacies, especially in relation to doing God's work?

~3~ Are you willing to allow God to work through you?

9
A Verification – 6:19-24

So Gideon went into his house and prepared a young goat and unleavened cakes from an ephah of flour. The meat he put in a basket, and the broth he put in a pot, and brought them to him under the terebinth and presented them. And the angel of God said to him, "Take the meat and the unleavened cakes, and put them on this rock, and pour the broth over them." And he did so. Then the angel of the Lord reached out the tip of the staff that was in his hand and touched the meat and the unleavened cakes. And *fire sprang up from the rock and consumed the flesh and the unleavened cakes.* And the angel of the Lord vanished from his sight.

Then *Gideon perceived that he was the angel of the Lord.* And Gideon said, "Alas, O Lord God! For *now I have seen the angel of the Lord face to face.*" But the Lord said to him, "Peace be to you. *Do not fear; you shall not die.*" Then Gideon built an altar there to the Lord and called it, The Lord is Peace. To this day it still stands at Ophrah, which belongs to the Abiezrites.

Judges 6:19-24

Need Proof!

Was it wrong for Gideon to have asked for a confirming sign? I do not think so! After all, as we see in this passage not only did God not rebuke him but He answered Gideon's doubts by providing a clear sign for him. Gideon wanted proof positive – and God graciously provided it.

Gideon had tried to talk God out of calling him but now he was sincerely seeking truth. "And he [Gideon] said to him, "If now I have found favor in your eyes, then *show me a sign that it is You* who speaks with me" (Judges 6:17).

Prepare for a Sign

Gideon asked for proof that it was God who was speaking to him. God responded with clear instructions.

"And the angel of God said to him, 'Take the meat and the unleavened cakes, and put them on this rock, and pour the broth over them.' And he did so" (Judges 6:20).

Sign Given

Gideon brought the meal back and offered it to the Lord. When the angel of God said to place the meal on a rock Gideon complied. Then the angel touched the meat and bread with his staff and it was instantly consumed by fire.

"Then the angel of the Lord reached out the tip of the staff that was in his hand and touched the meat and the unleavened cakes. *And fire sprang up from the rock and consumed the flesh and the unleavened cakes*" (Judges 6:21).

This miraculous sign should have been enough to convince Gideon, once and for all, that he was indeed dealing with the One True God.

Unfortunately, we see later that Gideon was still not fully convinced – this is the first of three miraculous tests.

What Now?

When Gideon realizes that he is really interacting with the Creator God, he becomes terrified. Now that he has seen the Lord directly, is he going to die?

"And Gideon said, "Alas, O Lord God! For *now I have seen the angel of the Lord face to face.*" But the Lord said to him, 'Peace be to you. *Do not fear; you shall not die.*"" (Judges 6:22b-23).

This verification that he was interacting with God allowed Gideon to recognize that his call came directly from God.

Peace

What a relief that he was not going to be struck dead. Gideon's response was worship including the building of an altar.

"Then Gideon built an altar there to the Lord and called it, *The Lord is Peace.* To this day it still stands at Ophrah, which belongs to the Abiezrites" (Judges 6:24).

"For He (Jesus Christ) Himself is our peace" (Ephesians 2:14a).

THINK AND GROW

Gideon was a reluctant leader who questioned the call of God. Gideon needed a personal encounter with God to gain assurance.

God does not despise nor refute honest doubt. God is compassionate and patient with us and our doubts. When Gideon struggled with doubts God did not give up on him.

God confirms His reality with His presence. He provides Gideon with both peace and purpose.

~1~ What insecurities and doubts do you have?

~2~ What excuses have you given yourself, and God, for why you won't serve Him more?

~3~ Gideon needed a personal encounter with God. If you have not had a direct encounter with God and the peace that comes with it, I invite you to do so right now!

"For *He Himself is our peace,* who has made us both one and has broken down in his flesh the dividing wall of hostility by abolishing the law of commandments and ordinances, that He might create in Himself one new man in place of the two, so making peace, and might reconcile us both to God in one body through the Cross, thereby killing the hostility. And He came and preached peace to you who were far off and *peace to those who were near.* For through Him we both have *access in one Spirit to the Father.* So then you are no longer strangers and aliens, but you are fellow citizens with the saints and members of the household of God, built on the foundation of the apostles and prophets, Christ Jesus Himself being the cornerstone, in whom the whole structure, being joined together, grows into a holy temple in the Lord. In Him you also are being built together into *a dwelling place for God by the Spirit*" (Ephesians 2:14-22).

~4~ Today believers have the advantage of the indwelling Spirit of God.

"If you then, who are evil, know how to give good gifts to your children, *how much more will the heavenly Father give the Holy Spirit to those who ask Him!*" (Luke 11:13).

~5~ If God calls you, He will go with you!

ACTION

67

10

Gideon's Worship – 6:24-27

Then *Gideon built an altar there to the Lord* and called it, *The Lord Is Peace*. To this day it still stands at Ophrah, which belongs to the Abiezrites. That night the Lord said to him, "Take your father's bull, and the second bull seven years old, and *pull down the altar of Baal* that your father has, and cut down the Asherah that is beside it and build an altar to the Lord your God on the top of the stronghold here, with stones laid in due order. Then take the second bull and *offer it as a burnt offering* with the wood of the Asherah that you shall cut down." *So Gideon took ten men of his servants and did as the Lord had told him.* But because he was too afraid of his family and the men of the town to do it by day, he did it by night.

Judges 6:24-27

Follow Directions

When the Lord is leading, He provides the specifics.

"That night *the Lord said to him*, 'Take your father's bull, and the second bull seven years old, and *pull down the altar of Baal* that your father has, and cut down the Asherah that is beside it and build an altar to the Lord your God on the top of the stronghold here, with stones laid in due order. Then take the second bull and offer it as a burnt offering with the wood of the Asherah that you shall cut down'" (Judges 6:25-26).

"Gideon selected ten men from his servants and *did exactly what God had told him*" (Judges 6:27a msg).

This was an act of worship and consecration unto the Lord.

Label It

Gideon built an altar right where he had been directed and called it *Yahweh-Shalom* or "The Lord is peace."

"Then *Gideon built an altar there to the Lord* and called it, *The Lord Is Peace*" (Judges 6:24a).

Obedience to God provides peace – an absence of strife.

Interestingly, in the Hebrew he called it *Jehovah-Shalom*, a name of God which occurs only in this one place.

~ Yahweh ~

Root meanings of *Yahweh* include "The Existing One" and "LORD." The concept is "to be" or "to exist." There is an underlying meaning of progressive revelation – a God who continues to reveal Himself. We have the option of intentionally increasing our knowledge of God and His nature.

~ Shalom ~

The meaning of *peace* in the Hebrew language includes concepts of flourishing, completeness (or wholeness) in all aspects of life. It includes safety and welfare. God is the source of all.

"In the Bible, shalom means universal flourishing, wholeness and delight — a rich state of affairs in which natural needs are satisfied and natural gifts fruitfully employed, a state of affairs that inspires joyful wonder as its Creator and Savior opens doors and welcomes the creatures in whom He delights."[12]

This concept of harmony is never dependent upon circumstances, but rather is dependent on complete trust in God.

"May the Lord of peace Himself give you peace at all times in every way. The Lord be with you all" (2 Thessalonians 3:16).

Peace

Gideon had just encountered God face-to-face and was no longer terrified of God. The title he gave to the altar: The-Lord-Is-Peace confirms this.

Quote

"When Gideon is fully at peace, what does he begin to do for God? If God loves you, he will use you either for suffering or service; and if he has given you peace, you must now prepare for war. Will you think me odd if I say that our Lord came to give us peace that He might send us out to war?" —Charles H. Spurgeon

THINK AND GROW

~1~ How would you rate your life today in regards to peace? (1—10)

~2~ If you rated below ten, do you think you may need to trust God more?

~3~ God wants our obedience, not to be granted favor with Him, but because we already have favor with Him.

~4~ A believer's spiritual health is sustained by regular worship. This may be the first time it is specifically mentioned that Gideon worshiped, but not the last (i.e., Judges 7:15). Not every detail of the lives of Biblical characters is included in Scripture, I am sure Gideon worshipped God many times more than are included in Scripture.

~5~ The last part of this chapter's passage states: "But because he [Gideon] was too afraid of his family and the men of the town to do it by day, he did it by night" (Judges 6:27b). Do you sometimes operate as a Secret Service Christian?

11

Down With Baal – 6:28-35

When the men of the town rose early in the morning, behold, *the altar of Baal was broken down, and the Asherah beside it was cut down*, and the second bull was offered on the altar that had been built. And they said to one another, *"Who has done this thing?"* And after they had searched and inquired, they said, *"Gideon the son of Joash has done this thing."*

Then the men of the town said to Joash, "Bring out your son, that he may die, for *he has broken down the altar of Baal and cut down the Asherah beside it.*" But Joash said to all who stood against him, "Will you contend for Baal? Or will you save him? Whoever contends for him shall be put to death by morning. If he is a god, let him contend for himself, because his altar has been broken down."

Therefore on that day Gideon was called Jerubbaal, that is to say, "Let Baal contend against him," because he broke down his altar. Now all the Midianites and the Amalekites and the people of the East came together, and they crossed the Jordan and encamped in the Valley of Jezreel. But *the Spirit of the Lord clothed Gideon*, and he sounded the trumpet, and the Abiezrites were called out to follow him. And he sent messengers throughout all Manasseh, and they too were called out to follow him. And he sent messengers to Asher, Zebulun, and Naphtali, and they went up to meet them.

Judges 6:28-35

Gideon had been obedient and built an altar to the One True God by precisely following the directions given him by God. Now God presents him with his first big mission.

Assignment

God had asked Gideon to tear down the altar of Baal that his father had built. Not only did this greatly offend his community but also his immediate family. But note that God is once again giving him a chance to obey Him.

This was the first big task that God assigned to Gideon.

~ Comment ~

As a young man I sometimes saw people head off to the mission field to be supported by those in their local church. The one thing that bothered me was that sometimes they had never shown any missionary traits or efforts at home before leaving for the mission field. In the example before us we see Gideon began his work for God among those closest to him.

The altar to Baal which his father had built was not a place to worship God – but to worship an idol of a false god. His family worshipped this idol and a tall pole had been erected for worship. This was all a significant indication of Israel's apostasy.

Asherah referred to a divine goddess, and the sacred wooden poles were located at places where she was worshipped.

Gideon carried out his God-given assignment under the cover of darkness. Jesus, speaking to His apostles, told them: "I am sending you out as sheep in the midst of wolves, so *be wise as serpents* and innocent as doves" (Matthew 10:16-17).

> "Now *the serpent was more cunning than any beast of the field* which the Lord God had made. And he said to the woman, 'Has God indeed said, "You shall not eat of every tree of the garden"'?" (Genesis 3:1).

As you would expect, once the Israelites realized it was Gideon who had done this to their idols, they were angry with Gideon.

Gideon had been obedient to what the Lord told him to do. It was an effort to purify his family and nation of their wickedness.

Idols

Question: What constitutes an idol?

Answer: Anything that comes between you and God.

Elimination of idols is extremely important:

"Who shall ascend the hill of the Lord? And who shall stand in His holy place? He who has clean hands and a pure heart, *who does not lift up his soul to what is false* and does not swear deceitfully. He will receive blessing from the Lord and righteousness from the God of his salvation. Such is the generation of those who seek Him, who seek the face of the God of Jacob" (Psalm 24:3-6).

God called Gideon to pull down the altar of Baal and cut down the Asherah poles (Judges 6:25-26). Then Gideon was to set up an altar to the Lord and sacrifice a bull, using the wood from the Asherah poles.

God's first task for Gideon was to get his own house in order before doing the greater things He would call him to do.

Culprit Found

"And they said to one another, *'Who has done this thing?'* And after they had searched and inquired, they said, *'Gideon the son of Joash has done this thing.'* Then the men of the town said to Joash, *'Bring out your son, that he may die*, for he has broken down the altar of Baal and cut down the Asherah beside it'" (Judges 6:29-30).

Gideon knew he was going to make his own people mad at him for doing this. He destroyed the altar at night so that no one would know who was responsible.

But what Gideon had done in the darkness of night did not stay concealed for long. When the community figured out that Gideon was the one who had destroyed their altars, they were outraged. They then went to Gideon's father and called for Gideon's death.

Dad Defends

"'Bring out your son, that he may die, for he has broken down the altar of Baal and cut down the Asherah beside it.' But Joash said to all who stood against him, *'Will you contend for Baal? Or will you save him?* Whoever contends for him shall be put to death by morning. *If he is a god, let him contend for himself, because his altar has been broken down*'" (Judges 6:30b-31).

Gideon's father made a very logical, common-sense argument for preserving his son's life. Since Baal was the offended party, he could defend himself. If Baal is truly a god, let him plead for himself, because his altar has been torn down. As a god he should be able to take care of this matter for himself.

New Name

Joash changed Gideon's name to Jerubbaal which is sometimes interpreted as *"let Baal plead."*

Gideon had earned the new name Jerubbaal (or Jerub-Baal) after destroying his family's idols to the false God.

"Therefore on that day *Gideon was called Jerubbaal*, that is to say, *'Let Baal contend against him,'* because he broke down his altar" (Judges 6:32).

Jerubbaal is a combination of two Hebrew words: the first is *riyb* or *rub*, which means literally "to grapple" and holds the figurative meaning "to wrangle" or "to hold a controversy." The second is the proper noun *Baal*, the name of the Phoenician god that Gideon picked a fight with.

Later in the Book of Judges we find his new name still being used (i.e., Judges 7:1, 8:29, 9:1).

"The name Jerubbaal means, 'A man against whom Baal is to strive and contend; a title of honor.'" —John Trapp

The Trumpet

"But *the Spirit of the Lord clothed Gideon, and he sounded the trumpet,* and the Abiezrites were called out to follow him. And he sent messengers throughout all Manasseh, and they too were called out to follow him. And he sent messengers to Asher, Zebulun, and Naphtali, and they went up to meet them" (Judges 6:34-35).

In the Old Testament the Spirit of God did not indwell believers like He does today. However, there are many incidents where the Spirit of God temporarily was with one of His believers.

Victory

As we have just seen, even when the enemy was present, the Spirit of God was with Gideon.

As we view this event in the life of Gideon – tearing down the family and community altars – we could almost consider it as a warm-up success for Gideon. He must have gained encouragement and increased confidence and faith having achieved the results that he did. Gideon was in the process of being changed by God from a timid fearful person into a "valiant warrior."

God was preparing him for much greater things to come. He will face much greater tasks in the future.

THINK AND GROW

Today, most Christians do not worship physical figurines or objects. However, I suspect that all Christians have had or do have idols. Anything that separates you from your deep love for your Savior is an idol.

~1~ Consider that Gideon was initially afraid to accept God's call but when he did, he was given a new name. In a similar way we are given a new name Christian, literally Christ-one.

~2~ Do you have something in your life which has become as important or more important than your relationship with God?

Gideon had idols and one of his biggest idols was *fear*. He feared the Midianites and what would happen to him if he was found working in his hiding place of the winepress. Like many of us, he feared that which his mind could not fully grasp – he feared the unknown.

~3~ What are your biggest fears?

~4~ Are there any fears that are causing you a restraint from deeper fellowship with God?

When God delivers a believer from the tyranny of idols, it is one of the greatest events a believer can experience. But He needs your cooperation.

~5~ What idols do you have to resist?

~ Image ~

Unfortunately, it is easy to worship the idol of our own image or reputation.

~ Materialism ~

In many communities the phrase "keeping up with the Joneses" is all too real. If our neighbor buys a new car, we need an equal or better new car to prove our worth.

~6~ Are possessions an addiction for you?

~ Addiction ~

There is the idol of addictions: alcohol, cigarettes, pornography, illicit sex, drugs, television, internet, social media, or even food or caffeine. How about fishing, hunting, or travel? Or what about a hobby or sport? Do you have as strong an affection for a sports team as you have for God?

The problem of all non-spiritual addictions is that they always end up not satisfying so the desire is always for more. It creates an endless search for satisfaction.

~7~ Do you have a current addiction?

~8~ If so, are you willing to admit it to yourself, then confess it to God, and then with His help conquer it?

Identifying idols is critical, but that is only the start to gaining victory. The next step is to tear down your idols.

~9~ What positive steps will you take to resolve it?

~Replacement ~

After Gideon had destroyed the idols, he offered a sacrifice in its place. Whatever idols are removed need to be replaced by something positive – or they will certainly return. Sacrifice and replacement are keys to victory.

It is a fact that we are unable to defeat the sin of idols simply by trying harder. We need God's help. We must replace the focus we have on the idol with a renewed love for God. We must rely on the Word of God and the Spirit of God combined with an attitude of constant prayer in order to gain and maintain victory.

"The weapons of our warfare are not of the flesh but have divine power to destroy strongholds" (2 Corinthians 10:4).

God's Word will always be indispensable in dealing with addictions: "I have stored up Your Word in my heart, that I might not sin against You" (Psalm 119:11).

"For the Word of God is living and active, sharper than any two-edged sword, piercing to the division of soul and of spirit, of joints and of marrow, and discerning the thoughts and intentions of the heart" (Hebrews 4:11-13).

"The Helper, *the Holy Spirit*, whom the Father will send in My name, *He will teach you all things*" (John 14:26a).

Also critical is constant communion with God – which is accomplished by continual prayer: "Rejoice always, *pray without ceasing*, give thanks in all circumstances; for this is the will of God in Christ Jesus for you. Do not quench the Spirit" (1 Thessalonians 5:16-19).

When Gideon made himself responsive to God, God guided him.

~ Sacrifice ~

Throughout the Old Testament sacrifice involved death. In a different but definite way, the New Testament carries out this same theme.

The Apostle Paul could say: "*I die every day* — I mean that, brothers — just as surely as I glory over you in Christ Jesus our Lord" (1 Corinthians 15:31 niv). The effective Christian life involves constant death to our will in order to accomplish God's will.

Sacrifice involves death to our will as a result of the realization of our brokenness. "The sacrifices of God are a broken spirit; a broken and contrite heart, O God, you will not despise" (Psalm 51:17).

~10~ Are there some aspects of spiritual sacrifice that you find easy?

~11~ What aspects of sacrifice are the hardest for you to submit to?

~12~ Can you explain the why of your two previous answers?

~13~ What specific idols do you need to tear down?

~14~ What are the specific steps you need to take to get right with God?

~ Comment ~

If you struggle in this area, there are resources readily available to you which have been helpful to many.

The Book of Ecclesiastes in the Old Testament records how the wisest man to live (King Solomon) also struggled. At the end of the book he concludes with a statement about what he had finally learned. "*The end of the matter; all has been heard. Fear God and keep His commandments, for this is the whole duty of man.* For God will bring every deed into judgment, with every secret thing, whether good or evil" (Ecclesiastes 12:13-14).

~ Editor's Notes ~

[1] Those who desire to finish their Christian life strong from this point on might want to consider the book: *"CHRIST'S DISCIPLE: How To Finish Strong," eBook ISBN: 978-1393844402, ASIN: B091XZF79B; or print edition ISBN: 979-8223262800, approximately 162 pages.*

[2] If you are having trouble knowing God's specific direction for your life, you might want to consider the book: *"GOD'S DESIRE FOR YOU: How To Please God,"* eBook ISBN: 978-1393211785, ASIN: B08H4F619W; or print edition ISBN: 979-8223962915, approximately 200 pages.

This book starts with the complex subject of the will of God presented in an innovative, easy-to-understand, and quick-read format that concisely explains the three main components of God's will. This is critical to understanding how to please God.

The illustrated "*Christian Life Model*" and "*Christian Guidance Model*" graphically display what God desires from His children and how they can be assured of making correct decisions throughout their lives. The book closes with a concise description of the benefits of following the two models.

12

Fleece Tests – 6:36-40

Then Gideon said to God, "If you will save Israel by my hand, as you have said, behold, *I am laying a fleece of wool on the threshing floor*. If there is dew on the fleece alone, and it is dry on all the ground, then I shall know that you will save Israel by my hand, as you have said." *And it was so*. When he rose early next morning and squeezed the fleece, he wrung enough dew from the fleece to fill a bowl with water.

Then Gideon said to God, "Let not your anger burn against me; let me speak just once more. *Please let me test just once more with the fleece.* Please let it be dry on the fleece only, and on all the ground let there be dew." *And God did* so that night; and it was dry on the fleece only, and on all the ground there was dew.

Judges 6:36-40

In a casual reading, it would appear that Gideon likes to test God. We have previously seen him test God with *meat and unleavened cakes* (Judges 6:19-24). Now we come to *two more* tests. What are we to understand from this?

I believe Gideon is sincerely seeking confirmation, proof if you will, that he is really dealing with God.

Fleece

In the English language today, one might speak of a fleecy cloud. A basic idea of fleecy is softness or fluffiness. Sometimes towels or sweatshirts are described as fleecy.

In this passage the word *fleece* comes from the fleecy nature of the wool of sheep. Today we are familiar with sheepskin rugs and sheepskin car seat covers. That is the essence of Gideon's fleece – essentially a piece of sheep skin with the wool still attached.

Now as a second test Gideon seeks more miraculous signs. The first night he asks God to allow the morning dew to affect only the fleece while keeping the ground dry. God provides such a result.

Still not fully convinced that it is really God he is interacting with, even after two miracles, Gideon asks for a third divine occurrence by reversing his request: cause the ground to be wet from the dew while the fleece stays dry. God does as he requests.

Gideon was using a typical bargaining method of "if you do this, then I will do this," or in Gideon's case, "I will know it is really You."

Motivation

I believe that Gideon was not questioning God's ability, power, or authority. He was trying to be certain that he was really dealing with God and that God would be with him. (Some other Biblical scholars think his motivation was quite different.)

Keep in mind Gideon was nervous – who wouldn't be? Was God really interacting directly with him?

Fear gripped him for at least two reasons. First, if he moved away from the false gods to the One true God, he would be at odds with his father.

Second, if he continued in his current direction, he would be angering God or His angel that he is involved with.

Still in doubt, Gideon was motivated to investigate further, so he thought through how he could become fully convinced. He decided on these two more miraculous tests.

His motivation was not in a contentious spirit or in arrogance. His motivation was to gain full confidence through confirmation from God. Based on God's reaction, I do not think God thought that Gideon was "dictating terms to Him."

Wet Fleece

"'If there is dew on the fleece alone, and it is dry on all the ground, then I shall know that you will save Israel by my hand, as you have said.' *And it was so*. When he rose early next morning and squeezed the fleece, *he wrung enough dew from the fleece to fill a bowl with water*" (Judges 6:37b-38).

Clearly, this was an obvious answer. It was not like the fleece felt a tiny bit damp but that Gideon was able to wring out the fleece and fill a bowl with the water while everything around was still dry.

Response

It is notable that Gideon did not keep his word to God. God had fulfilled his request about the fleece the first time—but he was still not convinced. In essence Gideon did not keep his word to God. Our God is understanding, patient, merciful, and gracious.

"This is an outstanding example of God's gracious patience with a troubled child." —Leon J. Wood

One would expect that at this point Gideon would have been convinced. Was he lacking faith or was it just not a super strong faith?

Remember the Gospel account of the father of a mute child: "Jesus said to him, 'If you can! All things are possible for one who believes.' Immediately the father of the child cried out and said, '*I believe; help my unbelief*'!" (Mark 9:23-24).

Dry Fleece

I believe Gideon had belief, but not enough for the circumstances. Consider his tone:

"Then Gideon said to God, '*Let not your anger burn against me*; let me speak just once more. *Please let me test just once more with the fleece. Please* let it be dry on the fleece only, and on all the ground let there be dew.' And God did so that night; and it was dry on the fleece only, and on all the ground there was dew" (Judges 6:39-40).

God granted this additional request for still another sign. Gideon was finally sure it truly was God whom he was dealing with. Now he knew that God was in fact calling him to be the one to deliver Israel from their current oppressors.

~ Reflect Back ~

"Then the Lord turned to him and said, '*Go in this might of yours, and you shall save Israel from the hand of the Midianites. Have I not sent you*?' So he said to Him, 'O my Lord, how can I save Israel? Indeed my clan is the weakest in Manasseh, and I am the least in my father's house.' And the Lord said to him, 'Surely *I will be with you, and you shall defeat the Midianites as one man.'* Then he said to Him, 'If now I have found favor in Your sight, then *show me a sign that it is You* who talk with me. Do not depart from here, I pray, until I come to You and bring out my offering and set it before You'" And He said, 'I will wait until you come back'" (Judges 6:14-18 nkjv).

Gideon was finally assured by the double fleece signs.

Symbolism

Symbolism within the Scripture is an area that sometimes causes significant disagreement. With that in mind, I merely offer a very brief overview of the probable symbolism in the Biblical account of Gideon and the fleece.

~ Fleece ~

Fleece represents God's sheep – which at that time were the Israelites who were following the law and the prophets.

~ Ground ~

The surrounding ground represents the Gentiles – they were surrounding the Israelites.

~ Dew ~

Water is symbolic of the Spirit of God (here and in other places in the Bible).

~ Wet Fleece ~

The dew that was wrung out into a bowl represents the doctrines of Christianity, which will be extracted from the Jewish laws and their interpretation. This foreshadows Christ pouring water into a bowl and then washing the disciple's feet.

~ Dry Fleece ~

The dryness of the fleece while the ground around was wet with dew represents the Jewish nation being put aside for a period of time, while the Gospel is preached to Gentiles.

Quotes

[1] "The fleece represents the Jewish people and the area around it represents the Gentiles. The fleece was covered with dew while all around was dry, representing the Jewish nation favored with the law and the prophets.

"The fleece was then dry and all around was wet with dew, representing that the Jewish nation was cast off for rejecting the Gospel and the Gospel was preached to the Gentiles and they converted to God.

"The dew wrung out into the bowl represents the doctrines of Christianity, which are extracted from the Jewish writings. This is also shadowed forth by Christ's pouring water into a basin and washing the disciple's feet" —Adam Clarke

[2] "Dew symbolizes God's reviving grace: Israel was heretofore the dry fleece, while the nations around were flourishing; now she is to become filled with the Lord's vigor, while the nations around lose it. The fleece becoming afterward dry while the ground around was wet symbolizes Israel's rejection of the gospel while the Gentile world is receiving the gracious dew. Afterward Israel in its turn shall be the dew to the Gentile world (Micah 5:7). Gideon pitched on a height at the foot of which the

fountain Harod ('the spring of trembling,' now perhaps Ain Jahlood) sprang. Midian pitched in the valley of Jezreel (Judges 6:33).

"The sign itself was to manifest the strength of divine assistance to his weakness of faith. Dew, in the Scriptures, is a symbol of the beneficent power of God, which quickens, revives, and invigorates the objects of nature when they have been parched by the burning heat of the sun's rays."[13]

Concluding Thoughts

We should not criticize Gideon's apparent lack of faith. The challenge he had been presented was massive – to deliver his people from the tyranny of the Midianites. He was an insignificant man in a scared village. How might you or I react if called upon in that situation? He had a weak faith – if in that situation I might have had no faith.

Faith is like a mustard seed which starts tiny and can grow to enormous size (Matthew 17:20).

We will later find that Gideon is called "a man of great faith" (Hebrews 11:32).

It was not a question of Gideon being stubborn, resistant, or unwilling to be used by God. It wasn't a questioning of God's ability to be with him and help him. It was a question of being sure he was interacting with God and not an imposter.

It would be stupidity for Gideon to fight the Midianites with his own strength. Was it really God who was seeking him out for this task? In those days direct interaction with God was a rare event – unlike today when the Spirit of God dwells inside each child of God.

Gideon required positive proof that it was the true God he was interacting with.

Many believe his fleece tests were because of a lack of faith. I believe that it was because of his developing faith that needed to be strengthened before he could act in faith in mighty ways.

If we act obediently in faith, even limited faith, God will honor our faith and provide encouragement and strength for the tasks He assigns us.

Gideon took some convincing, but he was acting out of faith and trust that if it was really God who he was communicating with, God would respond lovingly and graciously.

THINK AND GROW

Some new believers immediately make a complete turnaround and others grow slowly. Gideon was of the latter kind and did not quickly accept God's call. It took time and signs for him to be convinced. But God is always willing to work with those who are sincere in their faith – no matter how strong that faith is. God will increase our faith.

Recall that Moses reacted somewhat like Gideon when God was calling him. Both Moses and Gideon were looking inward at their own strength instead of upwards for divine strength. The problem was they were both focused on the "why not" versus the "how to."

~ Compare Moses' Reaction ~

"But Moses said to God, '*Who am I* that I should go to Pharaoh and bring the children of Israel out of Egypt?' He [God] said, '*But I will be with you*'" (Exodus 3:11-12a).

"And he [Gideon]said to Him, 'Please, Lord, how can I save Israel? Behold, *my clan is the weakest in Manasseh, and I am the least* in my father's house.' And the Lord said to him, '*But I will be with you*'" (Judges 6:15-16a).

The secret in both their situations was "*But I will be with you.*"

Remember that weak faith is always far better than no faith. God is patient with us even when we find it hard to trust Him.

God responds positively to honest doubt. "And God did so that night; and it was dry on the fleece only, and on all the ground there was dew" (Judges 6:40).

Was it pretty ugly for Gideon to ask a total of three times for a miracle to demonstrate it was really God? God did not despise Gideon nor reprimand him for his multiple requests – no, He responded to him positively. God rewards honesty even if it is honest doubt – He never asks His children to walk in blind faith. He desires that we learn of Him and, as we do, that we become increasingly obedient to the truth that He gives us.

Maybe Gideon had a great faith in God but just lacked confidence it was God whom he was interacting with.

"This is an outstanding example of God's gracious patience with a troubled child." —Leon J. Wood

God is not only willing but wanting to increase our faith.

It is okay for us to seek clarification from God when trying to understand His desires for us.

- We can be sure that God will never direct us in a way which is contradictory to His Word.
- Pray earnestly and constantly until God makes His path for you clear.
- Counsel from *mature* Christians can be helpful.
- Our problem often stems from our desire to hang on to something or bring something of our own strength to solve the issue. God is basically saying "you and I are the majority."

[1] Have you ever felt God's calling and resisted it?

[2] Do you find it scary to have to rely on God for a planned accomplishment?

[3] Have you ever tried to strike a deal with God? (i.e., "If You get me out of this situation, then I will serve You all the rest of my life.")

[4] Are you prepared for significant spiritual battle should the Lord call you? If not, perhaps you should study the armor of God (as listed in Ephesians 6:10-20).

~ *Putting Out the Fleece* ~

[5] This portion of Scripture is not meant to be an example that believers today should follow.

[6] Putting out a fleece is usually a poor decision-making method.

[7] Did Gideon sin in asking for a sign?

[8] Likewise, what about Thomas in the New Testament who also had doubts and, like Gideon, insisted on a sign.

"Now Thomas, one of the Twelve, called the Twin, was not with them when Jesus came. So the other disciples told him, 'We have seen the Lord.' But he said to them, '*Unless I see in His hands the mark of the nails, and place my finger into the mark of the nails, and place my hand into His side, I will never believe'"* (John 20:24-25).

The subject of using fleece tests today is our next chapter!

13

Fleece Today? – Jeremiah 29:11-14a

For I know the plans I have for you, declares the Lord, plans for wholeness and not for evil, to give you a future and a hope. Then *you will call upon Me* and come and pray to Me, and *I will hear you. You will seek Me and find Me.* When you seek Me *with all your heart, I will be found by you*, declares the Lord.

Jeremiah 29:11-14a

Should a Christian "put out the fleece" today? Bible scholars and theologians hold to various positions regarding this question. Let's briefly look at some rationale.

No

Those who hold this view may draw principles from passages such as, "*You shall not put the Lord your God to the test*, as you tested him at Massah" (Deuteronomy 6:16).

And in the New Testament we read, "Jesus, aware of their malice, said, '*Why put me to the test*, you hypocrites'?" (Matthew 22:18-19).

Should we ask the God for a sign? The short answer is there is no need, since God reveals His will clearly to us in His Word. We also have the Spirit of God indwelling us who guides us into truth and its application.

Jesus told His disciples, "When the Spirit of truth comes, He will guide you into all the truth" (John 16:13a).

Yes

Those who hold this view may draw principles from passages such as, "For I the Lord do not change" (Malachi 3:6a), or "Every good gift and every perfect gift is from above, coming down *from the Father of lights with whom there is no variation or shadow due to change*" (James 1:17b). If God honored Gideon's tests, will He not honor our sincere tests today?

"Jesus Christ is the same yesterday, today, and forever" (Hebrews 13:8).

There is no evidence that God was bothered or discouraged by Gideon's repeated requests that He prove Himself as God. There is also no evidence that God began to think He had made a mistake in choosing Gideon for the task.

Perhaps

Those who hold this view may draw principles from passages such as, "Without faith it is impossible to please Him, for whoever would draw near to God must believe that He exists and that He rewards those who seek Him" (Hebrews 11:6-7). Then later in this same Hall of Faith chapter we find that Gideon is specifically mentioned in verse 32.

Clarification

I believe that in our day the answer is that it is usually wrong to test God by "putting out the fleece." However, I also believe that God always honors true seeking, questioning, and the effort to find the truth.

How can fleece be only occasionally correct in our day? It is a matter of the heart!

"The Lord said to Samuel, 'Do not look on his appearance or on the height of his stature, because I have rejected him. For the Lord sees not as man sees: man looks on the outward appearance, but *the Lord looks on the heart*'" (1 Samuel 16:7-8).

When the fleece is put out, is it to prove there is no God? Or, when the fleece is put out, is it in a sincere attempt to find the truth about whether God is real or not?

THINK AND GROW

Importantly, putting out the fleece is not a tool for discovering God's specific will for your life.

Putting out the fleece may be appropriate at times of sincere and complete honesty in removing the doubts of whether God is really there and whether He is who He says He is. Doubts do not disqualify you from coming to a sincere faith in the One True God.

Gideon himself seemed to realize that testing God was not a good idea. For example, he asked God to not be angry with him for seeking a third sign (Judges 6:39).

But a key aspect that we learn from this account is how patient God is with us – even, perhaps especially, when we find it difficult to trust Him.

God is willing to stoop down and reassure us when we are afraid.

~1~ The unknown is scary and can easily make someone skeptical or afraid.

~2~ Prayer should always be the first step – and especially when facing the unknown.

~~~*~ In difficult situations in your past, has prayer been your first action?

~3~ God is willing to increase our faith if we are sincerely seeking the truth.

~4~ What do you think? Is "putting out the fleece" acceptable today?

~~~*~ Why or why not? If in a small group discuss.

~ Anecdote ~

My early childhood was a life of poverty. My dad had died just as I turned one year old. I had an older sister and brother. Mom continued to make sure we went to a solid Bible-believing church which was maintained throughout her life.

Following Mom's remarriage when I was eight years old, I got involved with the wrong crowd. At home I behaved well to avoid some of the problems my brother and sister had with my new father.

Fortunately, I escaped the wrong crowd by being accepted into an elite high school. But internally I remained a rebel in many ways including toward the Christian truths I had been taught throughout my childhood.

During my freshman year at the University of Washington I carried a heavy load which included 19 credit hours of engineering classes, being in the Air Force ROTC program, working 40 hours per week at the school's cyclotron, another part-time job with flexible hours, and also undergoing a difficult relationship. In reality, I had become an emotional wreck.

Beginning soon after entering university I came under heavy conviction by the Holy Spirit, but as an established rebel I fought all such convictions. I could easily write a substantial book about the many steps of rebellion in my life during that traumatic year at school.

One such resistance to God's call on my life involved my work at the university cyclotron.

> A cyclotron was an early machine in nuclear particle research. Its function was to accelerate charged particles such as electrons, ions, and protons to great speeds in a vacuum chamber. My role was as a statistician collecting, analyzing, and formatting the obtained data and then presenting it in useful form to the scientists. The end result was that the cyclotron was an essential part of experiments and resulting discoveries that shaped nuclear knowledge leading to advances in medicine and early atomic bombs.

I had a habit of going out to my car during breaks and listening to KGDN the local Christian radio station. One of those times I was under extremely heavy conviction and during the broadcast I was reminded of the Bible account of Gideon's experiences. With a sincere heart I decided to test for myself whether God was truly real.

My "office" in the cyclotron was in a rarely used darkroom with a red light above the door indicating when not to enter. In my time at work there I had never seen the red light turned on. I told God that if He was real, the red light should be on when I went back in to resume work. When I went back in, to my total astonishment, the red light was glowing brightly (similar to Gideon's first fleece test). In asking some of my coworkers, I was told it would be on for a few hours.

Back at my car I started the engine since I could not do my work. Then I suddenly turned the car off and told God that coincidences do occur in life and that I was headed back in and if He was real, the light would be off now. I went in and the light was off (similar to Gideon's second fleece test).

Looking back, I am ashamed to admit that I was more stubborn than Gideon – it took weeks until one evening in May at 18 years of age I went out on the balcony of my apartment, knelt down, looked up into the starry sky, and invited God to come into my life. The best decision of my life.

> "And Jesus asked his father, 'How long has this been happening to him?' And he said, 'From childhood. And it has often cast him into fire and into water, to destroy him. But if you can do anything, have compassion on us and help us. And Jesus said to him, 'If you can! *All things are possible for one who believes.*' Immediately the father of the child cried out and said, '*I believe; help my unbelief*'!" (Mark 9:21-24).

~5~ Have your thoughts about "putting out the fleece" changed after reading and reflecting upon this chapter?

14

Downsizing – 7:1-3

Then Jerubbaal (that is, Gideon) and all the people who were with him rose early and encamped beside the spring of Harod. And the camp of Midian was north of them, by the hill of Moreh, in the valley. The Lord said to Gideon, "The people with you are too many for Me to give the Midianites into their hand, *lest Israel boast over me, saying, 'My own hand has saved me.'*

Now therefore proclaim in the ears of the people, saying, '*Whoever is fearful and trembling, let him return home* and hurry away from Mount Gilead.'" Then 22,000 of the people returned, and 10,000 remained.

Judges 7:1-3

There is an American saying, "There are too many cooks in the kitchen." Or, have you ever heard one of the multiple jokes about "How many people does it take to..."

One example is, "How many people does it take to change a lightbulb?" I've heard various answers to this one, for example: "One person to get a ladder, one person to climb the ladder and hold the light bulb steady, and four people to turn the ladder so the bulb gets screwed into its socket."

How about you? In real life experience, have you ever experienced too many people for a job? God is about to begin to teach Gideon that he has too many soldiers for the task before him.

Process

There is a process at work. God is sovereign and He is working His plan which could be likened to the process for making steel.

~ Ore ~

The creation of steel begins by mining iron ore from the earth. It could remind us how "the Lord God formed the man of dust from the ground and breathed into his nostrils the breath of life, and the man became a living creature" (Genesis 2:7).

~ Iron ~

This iron *ore is processed into iron* through a fiery process. This could be likened to a human being moving from unbeliever to believer.

~ Steel ~

In order *to become steel, the iron must pass through another fiery process.*

"Beloved, *do not be surprised at the fiery trial when it comes upon you to test you,* as though something strange were happening to you. But rejoice insofar as you share Christ's sufferings, that you may also rejoice and be glad when His glory is revealed" (1 Peter 4:12-13).

~ Strength ~

In order *to become much stronger, steel is often passed through additional fiery processes* through a process called tempering.

Next Step

It took a couple of days after his fleece experience for Gideon to be convinced that he was really dealing with God, but he had come around and was now ready to trust God and His directions to him. Gideon was a farmer, not a soldier, but he now assembled a large army.

However, God had different plans. And it would involve additional testing and strengthening of Gideon.

But now the next big step for Gideon. God directs him to send home any of the soldiers he has assembled who are afraid to head into this coming battle.

~ Anecdote ~

The day I was inducted into the U.S. Army an interesting event occurred. There were 28 of us being inducted that day. Just before the induction ceremony the officer in charge stated that if there was any reason anyone should not be inducted into the military, they should take two steps forward. One big man about 6'4" with a very muscular build stepped forward. When asked about his reasoning he replied, "I'm a coward!" It was hard to keep from laughing. But to my surprise he was dismissed from our group and was taken to an office.

Great Reduction

Gideon had assembled an army of 32,000 soldiers prepared to carry out the planned attack. But God have different plans. When given a choice to return home because of fear and skip the war 22,000 readily did so. This was nearly a seventy percent reduction in his troops.

Imagine the thoughts Gideon must have had. He had followed God's instructions and assembled what he considered a reasonable army for the task, only to find out it was not acceptable to God. It would probably seem like being knocked out in the first round of a long fight.

Nervous

This incident caused Gideon to become very nervous and he asked God for another sign, which we explore in our next chapter.

THINK AND GROW

God's purpose in this downsizing was to prevent Gideon and his men from boasting.

God does not like man boasting about accomplishments when it is God Who accomplishes it through Him. "The people with you are too many for me to give the Midianites into their hand, *lest Israel boast over Me, saying, 'my own hand has saved me'*" (Judges 7:2b). Wouldn't this be the typical human reaction?

Also, God values quality over quantity – in God's economy quality always trumps quantity.

~1~ God uses ordinary people to accomplish His plans. He sometimes puts people into very difficult positions and uses their situations for His glory. He continues to do so today.

~2~ Gideon, and we, will only be successful when we are both humble and obedient.

~3~ If we are big in our own eyes, we are not useful for God's purposes. Do you think there may have been times when your personal pride got in the way of God's desires for you?

~4~ The key to humility is to switch our focus from our situation to God. Keep our eyes on Him. Remember how Nebuchadnezzar could say:

"At the end of that time, I, Nebuchadnezzar, *raised my eyes toward heaven, and my sanity was restored.* Then I praised the Most High; I honored and glorified Him who lives forever. ... At the same time that *my sanity was restored,* my honor and splendor were returned to me for the glory of my kingdom. My advisers and nobles sought me out, and I was restored to my throne and became even greater than before" (Daniel 4:34, 36-37 niv).

~ Editor's Note ~

The author has written a book about the issue of pride in the life of a believer: *"PRIDE: Good and Bad,"* eBook ISBN: 979-8201002053, ASIN: B09SGSQLH9; or print edition ISBN: 979-8223938781, approximately 158 pages.

15

A Few Good Men – 7:4-8

And the Lord said to Gideon, "*The people are still too many*. Take them down to the water, and I will test them for you there, and anyone of whom I say to you, 'This one shall go with you,' shall go with you, and anyone of whom I say to you, 'This one shall not go with you,' shall not go."

So he brought the people down to the water. And the Lord said to Gideon, "Every one who laps the water with his tongue, as a dog laps, you shall set by himself. Likewise, every one who kneels down to drink." And the number of *those who lapped, putting their hands to their mouths, was 300 men*, but all the rest of the people knelt down to drink water. And the Lord said to Gideon, "*With the 300 men who lapped I will save you and give the Midianites into your hand, and let all the others go every man to his home;*"

So the people took provisions in their hands, and their trumpets. And he sent all the rest of Israel every man to his tent, but *retained the 300 men*. And the camp of Midian was below him in the valley.

Judges 7:4-8

Downsizing Again

Gideon had drastically reduced his troops by about seventy percent. He must have expected to go to battle with those remaining 10,000 troops.

Now the next big surprising test. God was telling him to reduce his army's size even more. Gideon was to take them down to a brook and observe how they drank water. If they used their hands to form a cup and then drank from their hands they were to be kept. Others who lapped the water directly on their knees like a dog were to be released. Only 300 remained.

What was God's reasoning? I don't know. Do we need to understand His reasoning? No. Perhaps it was because while those down on all fours were more vulnerable, those drinking from their hands were more likely to be aware of their surroundings and any potential advancing enemies. If this was the reason, it may indicate they were wiser and more war-savvy than the others.

If this is the correct understanding, it was an issue of separating out those who were watchful from those who were not. While drinking from your hands you can still see around and even out to the horizon. Today believers are all part of the Christian army and commanded to be constantly alert.

"Be sober-minded; *be watchful*. Your adversary the devil prowls around like a roaring lion, seeking someone to devour" (1 Peter 5:8).

Jesus told Peter, "Watch and pray that you may not enter into temptation" (Matthew 26:41).

And consider this verse: "*Watch therefore, and pray always* that you may be counted worthy to escape all these things that will come to pass, and to stand before the Son of Man" (Luke 21:36 nkjv).

In God's perspective, the 10,000 troops were still too many. God wanted a lean but constantly on-guard army for the important task ahead.

It is also clear that with only 300 remaining soldiers they must have had an increased knowledge that the war they were about to enter into could only be won with God's help. They would have to rely on Him, not only for strength but also for the winning strategy. Remember also that this small band of soldiers was being led by a farmer boy recruited from hiding for fear of the enemy.

Outnumbered

From 32,000 soldiers to 10,000 soldiers to now only 300 soldiers. Keep in mind that they were headed to fight a Midianite Army of 135,000. Gideon's Army would have been severely outnumbered.

Gideon's 32,000 Troops

- The Midianite Army numbered 135,000
- Gideon started with 32,000
- *Outnumbered by more than 4 to 1*

32,000 to 10,000

- Almost a 70% reduction
- 31.25% left to fight
- *Now outnumbered 13.5 to 1*

10,000 to 300

- Another additional 97% reduction
- Only 3% of the original 10,000 are left to fight
- *Now outnumbered by 450 to 1*

Overall: 32,000 to 300

- 99% plus reduction
- Less than 1% (0.9375%) remaining to fight
- About to fight 135,000 Midianites
- *Now outnumbered 450 to 1*

THINK AND GROW

Reading this section of the Book of Judges one would get the impression that God likes subtraction or reduction. Perhaps this is to create right thinking in understanding the battle is the Lord's and that we can only win through His strength rather than our own. We need to be in *constant* awareness of our need for Him to control our situations. We need to be walking *with* Him at all times.

~1~ Have you experienced a time in your life when your "Plan A" fell apart forcing you to recognized your total dependence upon God?

~2~ Have you had times when you faced what seemed to be overwhelming obstacles?

~3~ Do you understand that any victories in your life are hopeless unless you are fully dependent upon God?

~4~ In your past victories over major obstacles have you recognized God's critical role?

~~~a~ Have you recognized God's strength and power on your behalf?

~~~b~ Have you recognized God's compassion and mercy on your behalf?

16
Victory Prophesied – 7:9-14

That same night the Lord said to him, "*Arise, go down against the camp, for I have given it into your hand.* But if you are afraid to go down, go down to the camp with Purah your servant. And you shall hear what they say, and afterward your hands shall be strengthened to go down against the camp." Then he went down with Purah his servant to the outposts of the armed men who were in the camp. And *the Midianites and the Amalekites and all the people of the East lay along the valley like locusts in abundance, and their camels were without number, as the sand that is on the seashore in abundance.*

When Gideon came, behold, a man was telling a dream to his comrade. And he said, "Behold, I dreamed a dream, and behold, *a cake of barley bread tumbled into the camp of Midian* and came to the tent and struck it so that it fell and turned it upside down, so that the tent lay flat." And his comrade answered, "This is no other than the sword of Gideon the son of Joash, a man of Israel; *God has given into his hand Midian and all the camp.*"

Judges 7:9-14

Barley Loaf

"Behold, I dreamed a dream, and behold, *a cake of barley bread* tumbled into the camp of Midian and came to the tent and struck it so that *it fell and turned it upside down, so that the tent lay flat*" (Judges 7:13b).

A cake of barley bread is made from barley flour which comes from barley grain. It has been dated to ancient times. It is gluten free. It was the bread of the poor – perhaps symbolic of Gideon's poor background and of Israel being very much the underdog army.

Remember the account of Jesus feeding the 5,000 where we read, "There is a boy here who has *five barley loaves* and two fish, but what are they for so many?" (John 6:9). Barley was the lowest of bread.

Passage Overview

I like the way this passage of Scripture is written in The Living Bible:

> "So after Gideon had collected all the clay jars and trumpets they had among them, he sent them home, leaving *only three hundred men with him.*
>
> "During the night, with the Midianites camped in the valley just below, the Lord said to Gideon, 'Get up! *Take your troops and attack the Midianites, for I will cause you to defeat them!* But if you are afraid, first go down to the camp alone – take along your servant Purah if you like – and listen to what they are saying down there! You will be greatly encouraged and be eager to attack!'
>
> "So he took Purah and crept down through the darkness to the outposts of the enemy camp. *The vast armies of Midian, Amalek, and the other nations of the Mideast were crowded across the valley like locusts – yes, like the sand upon the seashore – and there were too many camels even to count!* Gideon crept up to one of the tents just as a man inside had wakened from a nightmare and was telling his tent-mate about it.

"'I had this strange dream,' he was saying, 'and there was this *huge loaf of barley bread that came tumbling down into our camp. It hit our tent and knocked it flat!'*

"The other soldier replied, *'Your dream can mean only one thing! Gideon, the son of Joash, the Israeli, is going to come and massacre all the allied forces of Midian'*!" (Judges 7:8-14 tlb).

Meaning

What could a lowly barley loaf crushing Israel's foes tents mean? The unnamed Midianite soldier understood! *"Your dream can mean only one thing! Gideon, the son of Joash, the Israeli, is going to come and massacre all the allied forces of Midian!"*

The barley loaf, the poor man's bread, was symbolic of Gideon. The tent was likely the Midianites command tent. It was prophesying a vastly outnumbered Israelite Army would win the coming battle.

This was the encouragement Gideon must have needed at this point. It is like God was giving Gideon a fourth sign!

How did Gideon respond? He worshipped God. After thanking and praising God, he arose with new confidence and returned to his meager (in size) Army.

Result

If you were Gideon in this situation, how would you feel? He must have felt more confident that God was with him and would help him gain the victory.

Gideon has progressed from a scared wimp hiding as he threshes wheat to the captain of an army striking fear into a greatly larger enemy army. He hadn't entered into battle yet but the enemy is already beginning to fear him.

He went from *"my clan is the weakest in Manasseh, and I am the least in my father's house"* (Judges 6:15) to *"a mighty man of valor"* (Judges 6:12) in the view of the opposition, just as the angel of the Lord had described him.

One way God is sovereign is that He prepares the way for us. God was with Gideon, his small band of soldiers, and the Israelites.

THINK AND GROW

As we read the historical account of Gideon's life, we clearly see that he learned to trust God step by step. It was clearly a progressive thing.

Even though Gideon was afraid, he was willing to obey God.

Farm boy Gideon was an unlikely war hero. He was a reluctant warrior. But God was preparing him for a great war victory.

God will never ask us to do more than He equips us to do.

We are called into God's army and He provides for the battle.

The Christian warrior Apostle Paul near the end of his letter to the Ephesians wrote:

"Finally, be strong in the Lord and in the strength of his might. *Put on the whole armor of God,* that you may be able to stand against the schemes of the devil. For we do not wrestle against flesh and blood, but against the rulers, against the authorities, against the cosmic powers over this present darkness, against the spiritual forces of evil in the heavenly places. Therefore *take up the whole armor of God*, that you may be able to withstand in the evil day, and having done all, to stand firm. Stand therefore, having *fastened on the belt of truth*, and having put on the *breastplate of righteousness*, and, as shoes for your feet, having *put on the readiness given by the gospel of peace*. In all circumstances take up the *shield of faith*, with which you can extinguish all the flaming darts of the evil one; and take the *helmet of salvation*, and the *sword of the Spirit*, which is the Word of God, *praying at all times* in the Spirit, with all prayer and supplication. To that end keep alert with all perseverance, making supplication for all the saints, and also for me, that words may be given to me in opening my mouth boldly to proclaim the mystery of the gospel, for which I am an ambassador in chains, that I may declare it boldly, as I ought to speak" (Ephesians 6:10-20).

~1~ Are you fully prepared for whatever battles come your way?

~2~ Do you, like Gideon, take time to worship God as you see Him working in your life?

~3~ Are there any of the elements of spiritual warfare that Paul lists that might need strengthening?

17

Battle Preparations – 7:15-18

As soon as Gideon heard the telling of the dream and its interpretation, *he worshiped.*

And he returned to the camp of Israel and said, "Arise, for the Lord has given the host of Midian into your hand." And *he divided the 300 men into three companies and put trumpets into the hands of all of them and empty jars, with torches inside the jars.* And he said to them, "Look at me, and do likewise. When I come to the outskirts of the camp, do as I do. *When I blow the trumpet, I and all who are with me, then blow the trumpets also on every side of all the camp and shout, "For the Lord and for Gideon."*

Judges 7:15-18

Worship

We know that only small parts of the lives of Biblical characters are recorded in Scripture. It is notable that throughout history we see a consistent pattern of God's useful servants being worshipers. In Gideon's case we saw it previously demonstrated: "Then Gideon built an altar there to the Lord and called it, 'The Lord is Peace'" (Judges 6:24a).

In this passage we read, "As soon as Gideon heard the telling of the dream and its interpretation, he worshiped" (Judges 7:15a).

The dream interpretation Gideon had heard explained that God had already given the victory to Israel over their invaders – even though the physical battle had not yet started. This massive enemy army was already becoming fearful of Gideon and his small band. Gideon had this additional sign directly from God. Hearing the news, his immediate reaction was to bow and worship God.

No one will maintain their role as a spiritual leader in God's eyes for long without regular worship. Believers need to worship not only when God does especially great things in their lives but also on a regular basis as they live out their lives.

Ready for Battle

The battle is about to begin. An assessment of Gideon's army and equipment:

- 3 Companies of 100 men each
- Trumpets
- Torches inside jars

On the other side we find:

- 135,000 troops
- The troops are trained and equipped for the conventional warfare of the day
- Outnumbering Gideon's men 450 to 1

This certainly does not seem like an Army properly equipped and ready to win – let alone when greatly outnumbered. But importantly God had already let them know that He was with them and that they would win the battle.

Today we might also seem inferior to the forces we fight against, but Scripture tells us:

"For though we walk in the flesh, we are not waging war according to the flesh. *For the weapons of our warfare are not of the flesh but have divine power to destroy strongholds.* We destroy arguments and every lofty opinion raised against the knowledge of God, and take every thought captive to obey Christ, being ready to punish every disobedience, when your obedience is complete" (2 Corinthians 10:3-6).

We need to be sure we are fully equipped to fight spiritual warfare.

Being scared of our enemy is not the correct position for a believer – anymore than it was for Gideon. Timid Gideon had learned to trust, grow, and as a result became a mighty and valiant warrior for God. Gideon grew in his faith which gave him courage.

If your faith today is small, let it grow.

"The apostles said to the Lord, 'Increase our faith!' And the Lord said, 'If you had faith like a grain of mustard seed, you could say to this mulberry tree, "Be uprooted and planted in the sea," and it would obey you'" (Luke 17:5-6).

Note

Four times previously God had told Gideon he would be taken care of – yet Gideon was never confident. Now, a mere man tells Gideon things will be okay – and Gideon readily accepts it as fact.

"When Gideon came, behold, a man was telling a dream to his comrade. And he said, 'Behold, I dreamed a dream, and behold, a cake of barley bread tumbled into the camp of Midian and came to the tent and struck it so that it fell and turned it upside down, so that the tent lay flat.' And his comrade answered, 'This is no other than the sword of Gideon the son of Joash, a man of Israel; *God has given into his hand Midian and all the camp. As soon as Gideon heard the telling of the dream and its interpretation, he worshiped*" (Judges 7:13-15a).

THINK AND GROW

God can make the timid very confident.

Ministering close to home can be harder than ministering to those who don't know you. God asked Gideon to lead his own people in what seemed like an impossible task.

If you move forward in obedience in whatever small faith you have, God will honor you and increase your faith.

~1~ Do you regularly give thanks, praise, and worship to God as you live your life?

~2~ If you believe God created this immense universe, do you think there is any reason that He cannot supply all your needs?

Jesus said, "Your Father knows what you need before you ask Him" (Matthew 6:8b).

18

Battle Won – 7:19-25

So Gideon and the hundred men who were with him came to the outskirts of the camp at the beginning of the middle watch, *when they had just set the watch. And they blew the trumpets and smashed the jars that were in their hands. Then the three companies blew the trumpets and broke the jars. They held in their left hands the torches, and in their right hands the trumpets to blow.* And they cried out, "A sword for the Lord and for Gideon!" Every man stood in his place around the camp, and *all the army ran. They cried out and fled.* When they blew the 300 trumpets, the Lord set every man's sword against his comrade and against all the army. And *the army fled* as far as Beth-shittah toward Zererah, as far as the border of Abel-meholah, by Tabbath. And the men of Israel were called out from Naphtali and from Asher and from all Manasseh, and they pursued after Midian.

Gideon sent messengers throughout all the hill country of Ephraim, saying, "Come down against the Midianites and capture the waters against them, as far as Beth-barah, and also the Jordan." So all the men of Ephraim were called out, and *they captured* the waters as far as Beth-barah, and also the Jordan. And *they captured* the two princes of Midian, Oreb and Zeeb. *They killed* Oreb at the rock of Oreb, and Zeeb *they killed* at the winepress of Zeeb. Then they pursued Midian, and they brought the heads of Oreb and Zeeb to Gideon across the Jordan.

Judges 7:19-25

The Game Plan

~ Timing ~

"At the beginning of the middle watch, when they had just set the watch." The Bible is specific about the timing of Gideon's attack.

The middle watch is defined differently by scholars.

The most common understanding is that there were three watches of four hours each during the night – typically starting at 6:00 p.m., 10:00 p.m., and 2:00 a.m. In this scenario the battle began at 10:00 p.m.

The fact that the Bible is specific about the timing of the battle suggests that the time the battle started was important. It would have been in the dark and the opposing troops would have been tired from the day's activities and perhaps many were asleep. (Gideon's troops probably planned their rest knowing their plan of attack.)

~ Weapons ~

Gideon with his small band of soldiers was headed to war against a vast army of nomadic people who were the first people to use trained camels in war.

Nowhere does the Bible indicate that Gideon and his troops had any kind of normal war weapons. To the contrary their weapons were only trumpets, earthen pitchers, lamps, and most importantly they had God on their side.

Each of Gideon's men entered battle with a trumpet, a pitcher, and a torch. At the appointed time—about 10 o'clock at night.

The Attack

Perhaps the sound of 300 trumpets blasting into the air caused their opposing foes to think that there were 300 *companies* of soldiers attacking them.

Then Gideon's small band of soldiers smashed their earthen jars into pieces – it may have made quite the sound!

Next, the night was aglow with 300 burning torches piercing through the darkness.

The result was confusion in the Midianite army. They ran around trying to understand what was happening and were even fighting one another. In the dark they had trouble distinguishing their comrades from the Israelites – attacking their own fellow soldiers. Thousands of them died and the rest began to retreat and then flee from the scene.

"And *the army fled* as far as Beth-shittah toward Zererah, as far as the border of Abel-meholah, by Tabbath. And the men of Israel were called out from Naphtali and from Asher and from all Manasseh, and they pursued after Midian" (Judges 7:22b-23).

Finally, there was a uniform chorus of "the sword of the Lord and of Gideon."

The Result

Gideon's trumpets apparently woke the sleeping troops while confusing those troops who were awake on guard during the night.

I would imagine that Gideon was feeling a whole lot better. The overall account began with a scared and timid Gideon hiding from his enemies to becoming a valiant military leader striking fear into the Midianites and winning the battle over them.

Gideon and his men recaptured their fertile lands along the Jordan River.

In the aftermath Gideon, a most unlikely hero, had won the respect of his Hebrew people.

In summary, Israel's foes were completely routed, sustained massive losses, and fled the scene. Israel's homeland had been secured. It was a complete victory for Gideon acting with God's strength and blessing, and the result was that Gideon became a hero of Israel.

"Then the men of Israel said to Gideon, 'Rule over us, you and your son and your grandson also, for you have saved us from the hand of Midian'" (Judges 8:22-23).

Summary Quote

"300 trumpets blasted the air; 300 hands raised their earthen jars and smashed them to bits; 300 burning torches pierced the darkness; and 300 soldiers cried out, 'The sword of the Lord and of Gideon.'" —Hudson Tayler

Interesting

The timid little man who previously had been *hiding in a winepress* so the enemies would not discover him became aligned with God in contending first with Baal and then with Israel's enemies, the Midianites, along with other surrounding pagan nations. Later he would kill a key leader of their enemies in a wine press.

"The Angel of the Lord came and sat under the terebinth tree which was in Ophrah, which belonged to Joash the Abiezrite, *while his son*

Gideon threshed wheat in the winepress, in order to hide it from the Midianites" (Judges 6:11).

"They captured the two princes of Midian, Oreb and Zeeb. They killed Oreb at the rock of Oreb, and *Zeeb they killed at the winepress of Zeeb.* Then they pursued Midian, and they brought the heads of Oreb and Zeeb to Gideon across the Jordan" (Judges 7:25).

Lessons

God was true to His promises to an obedient Gideon, and God gave Gideon a very decisive victory over a vast enemy army.

God knows our weaknesses. He understands our fears and insecurities. God can use us in spite of our inadequacies.

God is willing to deliver us not only from the visible external trials, but also from internal idolatry and other hidden problems.

Like Gideon, we need to resolve our internal problems first.

God keeps His Word.

The little we have is enough when God is on our side and we are obedient. God can win victories with a fully committed minority.

Victory was Gideon's before the battle even started because it was God's war not Gideon's.

God wants you and me to live an obedient life of victory.

Since God has promised to be with us, we never enter spiritual battles alone. We should never doubt God.

God had observed Gideon's faithfulness by his obedience in taking a stand against his family and their idol worship. Later, Jesus said, "If you want to be My disciple, you must hate everyone else by comparison—your father and mother, wife and children, brothers and sisters—yes, even your own life. Otherwise, you cannot be My disciple" (Luke 14:26 nlt).

God commissions you to go forth and triumph in His name. "But the Spirit of the Lord clothed Gideon, and he sounded the trumpet, and the Abiezrites were called out to follow him" (Judges 6:34).

God values quality over quantity. God wants dedicated, disciplined, and obedient soldiers in His army. "The Lord said to Gideon, '*The people with you are too many* for me to give the Midianites into their hand, lest Israel boast over me, saying, "My own hand has saved me"' ... And the Lord said to Gideon, '*The people are still too many*. Take them down to the water, and I will test them for you there' ... And the Lord said to Gideon, '*With the 300 men who lapped I will save you* and give the Midianites into your hand, and let all the others go every man to his home'" (Judges 7:2-3, 4a, 7).

THINK AND GROW

No matter what odds you face, you can count on God's *presence*. "But now thus says the Lord, He who created you, O Jacob, He who formed you, O Israel: 'Fear not, for I have redeemed you; I have called you by name, you are Mine. *When you pass through the waters, I will be with you*; and through the rivers, they shall not overwhelm you; when you walk through fire you shall not be burned, and the flame shall not consume you. For I am the Lord your God'" (Isaiah 43:1-3a).

No matter what odds you face, you can count on God's *direction*. "Trust in the Lord with all your heart, and do not lean on your own understanding. In all your ways acknowledge Him, and He will make straight your paths" (Proverbs 3:5-6).

No matter what odds you face, you can count on God's *love*. "For I am sure that neither death nor life, nor angels nor rulers, nor things present nor things to come, nor powers, nor height nor depth, *nor anything else in all creation, will be able to separate us from the love of God* in Christ Jesus our Lord" (Romans 8:38-39).

No matter what odds you face, you can count on God's *purpose*. "And we know that for those who love God all things work together for good, for those who are called according to His purpose" (Romans 8:28).

God typically uses the weak and humble to accomplish His work. Gideon was weak and cowardly but God called him, commissioned him, and then used him mightily. By reducing his army down to just 300 men God allowed them to see that they could not win in their own strength. But working with God they could be delivered from the oppression of the Midianites. The victory was the Lord's not theirs.

"For consider your calling, brothers: not many of you were wise according to worldly standards, not many were powerful, not many were of noble birth. But God chose what is foolish in the world to shame the wise; God chose what is weak in the world to shame the strong; *God chose what is low and despised in the world,* even things that are not, to bring to nothing things that are, so that no human being might boast in the presence of God. He is the source of your life in Christ Jesus, whom God made our wisdom and our righteousness and sanctification and redemption. Therefore, as it is written, '*Let the one who boasts, boast in the Lord*'" (1 Corinthians 1:26-31).

~ Sidebar ~

It has been widely reported that a Queen of England loved this passage. Her comment was that she was so grateful for the letter "**m**" in this verse. She was glad that it says "not **m**any" as opposed to "not **any**"![14]

We see that Gideon had his own plans for his life but God intervened with a much more significant plan. "A man's heart plans his way, but the Lord directs his steps" (Proverbs 16:9 nkjv).

~1~ Are you letting others control your life or are you under the Spirit of God's control?

~2~ Like Gideon, have you sensed a direction from God and been troubled by doubt and fear?

~3~ Gideon sounded the trumpet at the beginning of victory. Someday – I believe very soon – many on earth will hear another triumphant trumpet. Will you hear it?

"In a moment, in the twinkling of an eye, at *the last trumpet. For the trumpet will sound*, and the dead will be raised imperishable, and we shall be changed" (1 Corinthians 15:52).

"This we declare to you by a Word from the Lord, that we who are alive, who are left until the coming of the Lord, will not precede those who have fallen asleep. For the Lord Himself will descend from heaven with a cry of command, with the voice of an archangel, and with *the sound of the trumpet of God*. And the dead in Christ will rise first. Then we who are alive, who are left, will be caught up together with them in the clouds to meet the Lord in the air, and so we will always be with the Lord. Therefore encourage one another with these words" (1 Thessalonians 4:15-18).

19

Resentment – 8:1-3

Then the men of Ephraim said to him, *"What is this that you have done to us*, not to call us when you went to fight against Midian?" And *they accused him fiercely*.

And he said to them, "What have I done now in comparison with you? Is not the gleaning of the grapes of Ephraim better than the grape harvest of Abiezer? God has given into your hands the princes of Midian, Oreb and Zeeb. What have I been able to do in comparison with you?" Then *their anger against him subsided* when he said this.

Judges 8:1-3

The Situation

Under Gideon's leadership Isreal had won an amazing victory over a massive army which was far better equipped than they were. They won by the hand of God.

Normal expectations would be that all would be worshipping God and rejoicing over their miraculous victory. Appreciation of Gideon and his leadership were in order.

However, as we know, mankind has a dark side inherited from Adam in his disobedience in the Garden of Eden. *"They accused him [Gideon] fiercely."*

"There is no distinction: for *all have sinned* and fall short of the glory of God" (Romans 3:22b-23).

"The Lord looks down from heaven on the children of man, to see if there are any who understand,

who seek after God. *They have all turned aside; together they have become corrupt; there is none who does good, not even one*" (Psalm 14:2-3; see also Psalm 53:3; Romans 3:10-18).

But there is good news in the free gift of salvation: "Come now, let us reason together, says the Lord: *though your sins are like scarlet, they shall be as white as snow*; though they are red like crimson, they shall become like wool. *If you are willing and obedient, you shall eat the good of the land*; but if you refuse and rebel, you shall be eaten by the sword; for the mouth of the Lord has spoken" (Isaiah 1:18-20).

With their natural sinfulness some of the men from Ephriam started complaining to Gideon! *"They accused him fiercely."*

~ Anecdote ~

At one time during my career, I was temporarily managing a small manufacturing company of about 125 employees. Many of the employees were relatively low paid and there were many complaints and concerns. As part of improving morale, I installed a free popcorn machine in the lunch room. Over time, complaints and concerns diminished. By the time I was done with my turn-around efforts for the company, the only complaints I was getting was the choice of which popcorn seasoning was available. One of the realizations I gained is that some humans will always find something to complain about – which is part of our Adamic nature.

The Ephraimites

Ephriam was the second son of Joseph – a founder of one of the twelve tribes of Israel.

Interestingly, the name Ephriam means "fruitful" or "fertile and productive."

In this passage the Ephraimites were envious and disappointed – maybe even feeling insulted – that they were left out and not directly involved in Gideon's victory. Most likely before the battle they were glad to not have to go to war. Perhaps they now worried they would be excluded from the spoils of war, including any allocation of the land that had been recovered.

Consider This Translation

"Now the Ephraimites asked Gideon, 'Why have you treated us like this? Why didn't you call us when you went to fight Midian?' And *they challenged him vigorously.*But he answered them, 'What have I accomplished compared to you? Aren't the gleanings of Ephraim's grapes better than the full grape harvest of Abiezer? God gave Oreb and Zeeb, the Midianite leaders, into your hands. What was I able to do compared to you?' At this, *their resentment against him subsided"* (Judges 8:1-3 niv).

The Response

God is able to give His followers the right words to say in difficult situations.

Speaking of future persecutions for His followers, Christ said, "And when they bring you before the synagogues and the rulers and the authorities, *do not be anxious about how you should defend yourself* or what you should say, for *the Holy Spirit will teach you in that very hour what you ought to say*" (Luke 12:11-12).

"A soft answer turns away wrath, but a harsh word stirs up anger" (Proverbs 15:1).

Gideon's Defense

"But he answered them, '*What have I accomplished compared to you?* Aren't the gleanings of Ephraim's grapes better than the full grape harvest of Abiezer? God gave Oreb and Zeeb, the Midianite leaders, into your hands. *What was I able to do compared to you?*' At this, their resentment against him subsided" (Judges 8:2-3 niv).

THINK AND GROW

~1~ Do you recognize your sinful nature which you inherited from the Fall of Man in the Garden of Eden?

~2~ Do you fully understand the verses quoted above which clearly state every person on earth is born with a sinful nature?

I often chuckle at people who think mankind is basically good. I figure they never had children!

"*Train up a child in the way he should go*; even when he is old he will not depart from it" (Proverbs 22:6). Have you ever met a child whom you suspected had never received any training?

~3~ Have you accepted the free gift of salvation from God due to His Son's substitutionary death on the Cross of Calvary?

~~~a~ If not, why not?

~~~b~ If not, why not do so right now?

Jesus explains His work for you this way:

"As Moses lifted up the serpent in the wilderness [providing salvation for those who chose it], so must the Son of Man be lifted up [on the Cross providing salvation for those who choose to accept His free gift], that whoever believes in Him may have eternal life. For God so loved the world, that He gave His only Son, that whoever believes in Him should not perish but have eternal life. For God did not send His Son into the world to condemn the world, but in order that the world might be saved through Him. Whoever believes in Him is not condemned, but whoever does not believe is condemned already, because he has not believed in the name of the only Son of God. And this is the judgment: the light has come into the world, and people loved the darkness rather than the light because their deeds were evil. For everyone who does wicked things hates the light and does not come to the light, lest his deeds should be exposed. But whoever does what is true comes to the light, so that it may be clearly seen that his deeds have been carried out in God" (John 3:14-21).

Your words in prayer to God are not critical, but your sincerity is!

20

No Food – 8:4-9

And Gideon came to the Jordan and crossed over, he and the 300 men who were with him, *exhausted yet pursuing.* So he said to the men of Succoth, *"Please give loaves of bread to the people who follow me, for they are exhausted,* and I am pursuing after Zebah and Zalmunna, the kings of Midian." And the officials of Succoth said, "Are the hands of Zebah and Zalmunna already in your hand, *that we should give bread to your army?"*

So Gideon said, "Well then, when the Lord has given Zebah and Zalmunna into my hand, *I will flail your flesh with the thorns of the wilderness and with briers."* And from there he went up to Penuel, and spoke to them in the same way, and the men of Penuel answered him as the men of Succoth had answered. And he said to the men of Penuel, *"When I come again in peace, I will break down this tower."*

Judges 8:4-9

Gideon's small band of 300 soldiers had accomplished a rout of the huge Midianite army – but some of them escaped as they fled. Gideon now leads his army in pursuit of the escaping Midianites headed for the wilderness. He is committed to hunting them down and destroying them, even if it takes him to the eastern side of the Jordan River.

Setting

Having fought a strenuous and out-numbered battle, Gideon's troops are hungry and exhausted. As Gideon passes through some towns of his own countrymen, he seeks food for his troops. But the response was not as one would expect.

The Message translates this passage this way: "Gideon and his three hundred arrived at the Jordan and crossed over. *They were bone-tired* but still pressing the pursuit. He asked the men of Succoth, 'Please, give me some loaves of bread for my troops I have with me. *They're worn out, and I'm hot on the trail of Zebah and Zalmunna, the Midianite kings.'*

~ Sidebar ~

"Gideon and his three hundred arrived..." confirms that none were lost in their horrific battle.

"But the leaders in Succoth said, '*You're on a wild goose chase*; why should we help you on a fool's errand?' Gideon said, 'If you say so. But when God gives me Zebah and Zalmunna, *I'll give you a thrashing, whip your bare flesh with desert thorns and thistles!*'

"He went from there to Peniel and made the same request. *The men of Peniel, like the men of Succoth, also refused.* Gideon told them, "*When I return safe and sound, I'll demolish this tower.*" (Judges 8:4-9 msg).

So Gideon said to the men of Succoth, '*Please give loaves of bread to the people who follow me, for they are exhausted, and I am pursuing after Zebah and Zalmunna, the kings of Midian.*"

~ Succoth ~

The geographical area of Succoth was east of the Jordan River and north of Jabbok. Succoth not only referred to the town but also to the surrounding valley (the valley is specifically mentioned in Psalms 60:6 and 108:7).

An interesting sidelight is that Succoth is also an alternate name for the Feast of Tabernacles, an eight-day Jewish harvest festival. It commemorates the Israelites' days of living in the wilderness.

~ Zebah and Zalmunna ~

Zebah and Zalmunna were both Midianite kings. Later we will find Gideon returning to them in revenge.

Food Refusal

Gideon pleads with the kings of these two Midianite towns for some food and water for his famished army. Instead of being quick to respond, the towns start asking clarifying questions. *"Are the hands of Zebah and Zalmunna already in your hand, that we should give bread to your army?"*

They had most likely seen some of the fleeing Midianite soldiers and in effect were saying, "You have failed and why should we help you and risk repercussion and retribution?" It appears they were fearful that Gideon had not been successful.

But by siding with the enemies of Israel, were they setting themselves up for judgement? In essence they were aiding and abetting Israel's enemies. This of course was putting Gideon and his troops in danger – as they moved on without any nourishment. They were already near exhaustion.

Gideon's Response

As a judge Gideon was the spiritual leader of the nation of Israel. During the time of the judges God often used judges to bring divine judgement on evil nations.

"So Gideon said, 'Well then, when the Lord has given Zebah and Zalmunna into my hand, *I will flail your flesh with the thorns of the wilderness and with briers.*' And from there he went up to Penuel, and spoke to them in the same way, and the men of Penuel answered him as the men of Succoth had answered. And he said to the men of Penuel, *'When I come again in peace, I will break down this tower'*" (Judges 6:7-9).

~ Penuel ~

The area of Penuel is found much earlier in Scripture.

"And He said, 'Your name shall no longer be called Jacob, but Israel; for *you have struggled with God and with men, and have prevailed.*' Then Jacob asked, saying, 'Tell me Your name, I pray.' And He said, 'Why is it that you ask about My name?' And He blessed him there.

"So *Jacob called the name of the place Penuel*: 'For I have seen God face to face, and my life is preserved.' Just as he crossed over Penuel the sun rose on him, and he limped on his hip. Therefore to this day the children of Israel do not eat the muscle that shrank, which is on the hip socket, because He touched the socket of Jacob's hip in the muscle that shrank" (Genesis 32:28-32 nkjv).

The name Penuel has come to mean "face of God" or "vision of God."

In our Judges passage Gideon had gone to a town called Penuel, which is not far from Succoth.

~ Review ~

Gideon has stated categorically, *"Well then, when the Lord has given Zebah and Zalmunna into my hand, I will flail your flesh with the thorns of the wilderness and with briers"* and he said to the men of Penuel, *'When I come again in peace, I will break down this tower."*

THINK AND GROW

One lesson is that we need to let go of things and resources which we cling to and instead trust completely in God.

Gideon's small fighting force was weak, tired, hungry, and exhausted, yet they were still pursuing and carrying out the mission God had given them.

Like Gideon and his men, we must carry on the mission God has given us regardless of the obstacles and conditions we face. How are you doing?

Let the Apostle Paul be our example:

"But whatever anyone else dares to boast of—I am speaking as a fool—I also dare to boast of that. Are they Hebrews? So am I. Are they Israelites? So am I. Are they offspring of Abraham? So am I. Are they servants of Christ? I am a better one—I am talking like a madman—with far greater labors, far more imprisonments, with countless beatings, and often near death. *Five times I received at the hands of the Jews the forty lashes less one. Three times I was beaten with rods. Once I was stoned. Three times I was shipwrecked; a night and a day I was adrift at sea; on frequent journeys, in danger from rivers, danger from robbers, danger from my own people, danger from Gentiles, danger in the city, danger in the wilderness, danger at sea, danger from false brothers; in toil and hardship, through many a sleepless night, in hunger and thirst, often without food, in cold and exposure. And,* apart from other things, there is the daily pressure on me of my anxiety for all the churches. Who is weak, and I am not weak? Who is made to fall, and I am not indignant? *If I must boast, I will boast of the things that show my weakness*" (2 Corinthians 11:21-31).

"But He said to me [Paul], 'My grace is sufficient for you, for my power is made perfect in weakness.' Therefore *I will boast all the more gladly of my weaknesses*, so that the power of Christ may rest upon me. For the sake of Christ, then, I am content with weaknesses, insults, hardships, persecutions, and calamities. *For when I am weak, then I am strong*" (2 Corinthians 12:9-10).

RESULTS

145

21

Victory – 8:10-12

Now Zebah and Zalmunna were in Karkor with their army, about 15,000 men, all who were left of all the army of the people of the East, *for there had fallen 120,000 men* who drew the sword.

And Gideon went up by the way of the tent dwellers east of Nobah and Jogbehah and *attacked the army, for the army felt secure.* And Zebah and Zalmunna fled, and he pursued them and *captured the two kings of Midian, Zebah and Zalmunna,* and *he threw all the army into a panic.*

Judges 8:10-12

Enemy Size

The enemy Midianite Army had been soundly defeated: 120,000 troops had been killed and now the remaining 15,000 were fleeing. The panicking Midianites were fearful, having seen so many of their fellow soldiers killed.

"By this time Zebah and Zalmunna were in Karkor with *15,000 warriors—all that remained of the allied armies of the east, for 120,000 had already been killed*" (Judges 8:10 nlt).

While this must have greatly encouraged Gideon's band, they were still outnumbered by a ratio of 50 to 1.

Strategy

The Midianite Army was scurrying to get across the Jordan River which they believed would make them far more secure.

Meanwhile Gideon was still holding on to his goal to fully accomplish the mission given to him by God and to fully conquer their current enemies. He is pushing on with determination.

"And *Gideon went up by the route of those who dwelt in tents east of Nobah and Jogbehah and smote their camp* {unexpectedly}, *for the army thought itself secure.* And Zebah and Zalmunna fled, and he pursued them and took the two kings of Midian, Zebah and Zalmunna, and *terrified all the army*" (Judges 8:11-12 amp).

It appears Gideon chose a longer route where he could expect a friendlier reception. I suspect he also considered this route to be unexpected – which could give him the additional advantage of surprise. He most likely expected more sympathy and a giving spirit from those living in tents than from those living in the walled cities. At any rate we read the *opposing army felt secure.*

Success

"Gideon circled around by the caravan route east of Nobah and Jogbehah, *taking the Midianite army by surprise.* Zebah and Zalmunna, *the two Midianite kings, fled, but Gideon chased them down and captured all their warriors*" (Judges 8:11-12 nlt).

THINK AND GROW

~1~ Remember that God chose Gideon who was the weakest man in a weak family of the smallest tribe in Israel. What might God be capable of doing with you?

One thing we see illustrated is that God does not depend on overpowering numbers to fight His enemies. He does depend upon faithful obedient servants.

~2~ Are you ready and willing to allow God to use you for mighty things?

"But God, being rich in mercy, because of the great love with which He loved us, even when we were dead in our trespasses, made us alive together with Christ — *by grace you have been saved* — and raised us up with Him and seated us with Him in the heavenly places in Christ Jesus, so that in the coming ages He might show the immeasurable riches of His grace in kindness toward us in Christ Jesus. For *by grace you have been saved through faith. And this is not your own doing; it is the gift of God, not a result of works, so that no one may boast.* For we are His workmanship, created in Christ Jesus for good works, which God prepared beforehand, that we should walk in them" (Ephesians 2:4-10).

A key word in this passage is *grace*. Grace is getting something good which we don't deserve. Therefore, when God chooses to use us, we have no basis for boasting.

"For who sees anything different in you? *What do you have that you did not receive? If then you received it, why do you boast* as if you did not receive it?" (1 Corinthians 4:7).

This pattern of God using unlikely humble people is found throughout the Word of God. Examples include David versus Goliath, the feats of Samson, and of course the Apostles Paul and Peter in the New Testament.

~3~ Are you willing to allow God to use you to the fullest extent He desires?

22

A Young Man – 8:13-14

Then Gideon the son of Joash returned from the battle by the ascent
of Heres. And *he captured a young man of Succoth and questioned him.
And he wrote down for him the officials and elders of Succoth,
seventy-seven men.*

Judges 8:13-14

Setting

The major battle with the Midianites is over. With God's power
Gideon has won and is returning victoriously. But two towns, Zebah
and Zalmunna, have refused help for his war-weary troops. Then
Gideon received the same response at Penuel. In both cases Gideon
promised revenge.

Gideon and his troops have taken a different route home. They have
gone around Penuel and back to Succoth. This surprise visit makes
it more likely he can punish the guilty without them escaping. On
arriving in the area, he takes captive a young man.

This man could write which could indicate that he had education and
was quite likely an official of some level. Gideon forces him to list
all the elders and officials of the town so that he can know who he
is looking for. He will then hold these 77 men responsible for the
decision not to provide aid to God's deliverer over the enemies of Israel.

Heres

Gideon returned from the major battle by climbing around Mount Heres. This mountain is also known as "Har-Heres" or "Mount Heres" (Judges 1:35), as well as "City of Heres" or "City of the Sun".[15] Other scholars translate the meaning as simply "the sun" or "Sun Mountain."

Some scholars believe it is the same as Mount Jearim (Ir-shemesh in Judges 1:35, also known as Beth-shemesh).

Before Sunrise?

Many translations indicate that Gideon was making his ascent in the dark before sunrise.[16] "Gideon son of Joash turneth back from the battle, *at the going up of the sun*" (Judges 8:13 ylt).

Another example is the Authorized Version which reads: "And Gideon the son of Joash returned from battle *before the sun was up*" (Judges 8:14 kjv).

Some scholars conclude that since the name of this mountain pass is connected with the *sun* that the passage is not necessarily connected with the rising of the sun. However other scholars maintain the literal translation. For example:

"This rendition may be well defended and gives excellent sense." —Hervey

"Without any doubt the word 'Heres' is an ancient word for 'sun'; and the foolish excuse for making this a proper name of some place is based totally upon what some scholar imagines to be the customary use of 'up' or 'ascent.' However, where is the scholar who knows *all* the uses of such words? Furthermore, when they have made a place-name out of it, *where* is the place? Of course, there is no such place. Furthermore, the mention of sunrise here indicates, what is almost a certainty, namely, that Gideon attacked the kings at Karkor *at night*. Is that not what he did previously? Why would he have changed his tactics?" —Albert Barnes[17]

Captured

Gideon *"captured a young man of Succoth and questioned him."*

"Captured" (*lakad*) is a word which typically was used in the context of seizing, catching in a net, trap, or pit. The context could be gaining control of a town, a population, a whole kingdom, or the spoils of the capture.

Information

The captured young man *"wrote down for him the officials and elders of Succoth, seventy-seven men."*

~ Notes ~

[1] It was not unusual to have the ability to write in that era. Writing was relatively common by the time of the Judges. First written documents date back to 3000 B.C. and written documents from Canaan have been found dating back to the fifteenth century.

"That this randomly encountered young man was literate strongly suggests that the Israelites in general were literate at this time, despite their previous decades of desert life and warfare." —Henry Morris

[2] Some scholars believe that this youth was probably a local official – one who was familiar with the men in leadership positions.

[3] This also makes it clear that Gideon could read.

[4] This is the first mention of elders in the Book of Judges. This was the form of civil government of the Israelites during this period.

[5] Succoth was a part of the tribe of Gad – which was across the Jordan River (Joshua 13:27). The ruins of Succoth are south of Beth-Shan.

[6] Being on the eastern side of the Jordan in Midianite territory, we can easily understand why they might be unlikely to reveal information which could cause retaliation from the Midianites.

[7] This list of 77 leaders was critical information.

"The written list would enable Gideon to punish the guilty and spare the innocent people. Succoth was governed by a Sanhedrim or council of *seventy elders* (compare Numbers 11:16), with perhaps seven others of superior rank called *princes*."[18] Some scholars believe the princes were the military leaders.

"The elders are heads of families; the princes (compare verse 6) are the military leaders."[19]

Who were the 77? Quite possibly the 77 were comprised of the Sanhedrin and seven high ranking military officers (princes).

THINK AND GROW

Negative: Gideon was reluctant and slow to believe God and be obedient to his calling.

Positive: Once Gideon was convinced it was God he was dealing with, he became a loyal and obedient follower.

As the historical account of Gideon continues, we see him become a strong leader for his nation. He displayed great courage and never backed down even when up against great odds against him and his men. He was willing to stand for God and His priorities when it was not a popular thing to do.

~1~ When you have experienced significant opposition to your spiritual beliefs, have you stood strong?

~2~ Are you willing to be thought foolish by doing what you know to be right?

~3~ What is the most significant thing to you about Gideon to this point?

23

Gideon's Revenge – 8:15-17

And he came to the men of Succoth and said, "Behold Zebah and Zalmunna, about *whom you taunted me*, saying, 'Are the hands of Zebah and Zalmunna already in your hand, that we should give bread to your men who are exhausted'?"

And *he took the elders of the city, and he took thorns of the wilderness and briers and with them taught the men of Succoth a lesson. And he broke down the tower of Penuel and killed the men of the city.*

Judges 8:15-17

Earlier the men of Succoth (Zebah and Zalmunna) and Penuel had refused to help Gideon with supplies for his troops (Judges 8:4-9) and Gideon had promised revenge. That time has come.

Taunted

"You taunted me." The word taunted (*charaph*) means to agitate, or reproach. It suggests jeering, mocking, scorning, or as we might refer to today as "in your face!" It is a defying, demeaning of or despising something or someone. It definitely carries with it more than a simple "no" because it is insulting.

Exhausted

Gideon's men *"who are exhausted."* His men were tired to the point of being faint. Yet the men of Succoth showed no compassion to these worn-out troops.

There is a subtle change of wording related to this incident. Earlier Gideon had asked, "Please give loaves of bread to *the people* who follow me, for they are exhausted" (Judges 8:5a). They replied, "give bread to *your army*?" (Judges 8:6b).

This indicates the insensitivity to the righteous battle Gideon was engaged in.

Disciplined

"He took the elders of the city, and he took thorns of the wilderness and briers and with them taught the men of Succoth a lesson. And he broke down the tower of Penuel and killed the men of the city."

While not directly related to Gideon, there is an interesting passage in Micah: "Their hands are on what is evil, to do it well; the prince and the judge ask for a bribe, and the great man utters the evil desire of his soul; thus they weave it together. The best of them is *like a brier*, the most upright of them *a thorn hedge*. The day of your watchmen, of your punishment, has come; now their confusion is at hand" (Micah 7:3-4).

Gideon is acting as a righteous Judge whom God has commissioned. He is also following through with his previous pronouncement.

Gideon had not asked much of them, just food and water for his weary battle-worn troops, but he was refused basic needs. He wasn't requesting victory parades or other forms of congratulations for a victory in a massively overmatched battle – just sustenance to finish the fight.

In a very real way, they were showing contempt for God who had raised up this small band of soldiers on Israel's behalf.

They had been warned of exactly what their punishment would be (Judges 8:7-9). In justice the punishment came.

The Punishment

"He took the elders of the city, and he took thorns of the wilderness and briers and with them taught the men of Succoth a lesson" (Judges 8:16).

Various translations describe the punishment with different wording. Here are a few samples.

"He took the elders of the town and taught the men of Succoth a lesson by *punishing them with desert thorns and briers*" (niv).

"He seized the leaders of the city, along *with some desert thorns and briers; he then 'threshed' the men of Succoth with them*" (net).

"Then he took the responsible men of the town and *had them crushed on a bed of thorns and sharp stems*" (bbe).

"He took the elders of the city, and *thorns and briers of the desert, and ground these men of Succoth into them*" (nab).

"He then seized the elders of the town and, *taking desert-thorn and thistles, tore the men of Succoth to pieces*" (njb).

"So he took the elders of the city and *he took thorns of the wilderness and briers and with them he trampled the people of Succoth*" (nrs).

~ Penuel ~

"And he broke down the tower of Penuel and killed the men of the city" (Judges 8:17).

That verse says it all!

THINK AND GROW

~ The Bad News ~

"All have sinned and fall short of the glory of God" (Romans 3:23).

"Be sure your sin will find you out" (Numbers 32:23b).

"How much worse punishment, do you think, will be deserved by the one who has spurned the Son of God, and has profaned [made common] the blood of the covenant by which he was sanctified, and has outraged the Spirit of grace? For we know Him who said, '*Vengeance is mine; I will repay.*' And again, 'The Lord will judge His people.' It is a fearful thing to fall into the hands of the living God" (Hebrews 10:29-31).

~ The Good News (Gospel) *~*

There is a solution for your sins.

"And so, from the day we heard, we have not ceased to pray for you, asking that you may be filled with the knowledge of His will in all spiritual wisdom and understanding, so as to walk in a manner worthy of the Lord, fully pleasing to Him, bearing fruit in every good work and increasing in the knowledge of God. May you be strengthened with all power, according to His glorious might, for all endurance and patience with joy, giving thanks to the Father, who has qualified you to share in the inheritance of the saints in light. He has delivered us from the domain of darkness and transferred us to the kingdom of His beloved

Son, in whom we have redemption, the forgiveness of sins" (Colossians 1:9-14).

But that Good News is only good if you are willing to accept the gift of salvation available to you.

24

Gideon Kills – 8:18-21

Then he said to Zebah and Zalmunna, "*Where are the men whom you killed at Tabor?*" They answered, "*As you are, so were they.* Every one of them resembled the son of a king." And he said, "They were my brothers, the sons of my mother. As the Lord lives, *if you had saved them alive, I would not kill you.*"

So he said to Jether his firstborn, "*Rise and kill them!*" But the young man did not draw his sword, for he was afraid, because he was still a young man. Then Zebah and Zalmunna said, "Rise yourself and fall upon us, for as the man is, so is his strength." And *Gideon arose and killed Zebah and Zalmunna,* and he took the crescent ornaments that were on the necks of their camels.

Judges 8:18-21

Description

"*Where are the men whom you killed at Tabor?*" They answered, "*As you are, so were they.*"

It can be paraphrased in this way: "*Describe for me the men* that you killed over near Mount Tabor. And they said, well *actually, they look sort of like you*, good-looking, they sort of look like sons of God."

Apparently Zebah and Zalmunna had massacred Gideon's family while he had gone to war against the Midianites. Gideon had heard some unverified and differing accounts of it, and now questions them about it. They, almost proudly, acknowledge it, and even describe the persons whom they slew, by which Gideon was able to determine that they were *his own brethren*.

"We learn that these kings had put the brothers of Gideon to death, and apparently not in open fight; but they had murdered them in an unrighteous and cruel manner. And Gideon made them atone for this with their own lives." —Keil and Delitzsch Commentary on the Old Testament

In an attempt to settle Gideon's anger these two worldly-wise kings flatter Gideon. They are essentially complimenting Gideon – the men that died were like you Gideon – implying that they have respect for the men who died.

Response

Gideon had previously made it clear that he would come back to "take care of business" (Judges 8:7-9). However, instead of doing the killing himself he delegates the task to his young first-born son Jether: *"Rise up and kill these fellows."* However, this boy quite likely a teenager who with little warfare experience, was intimidated and so he hesitated.

Perhaps Gideon's motivation of delegating to his young son was to add the disgrace of dying at the hand of a young boy.

"Then Zebah and Zalmunna said, *'Rise yourself and fall upon us, for as the man is, so is his strength'.*" In essence these two kings are mocking the young man for his lack of manhood – and subtly challenging Gideon's personal manhood.

Gideon Takes Action

"Then Zebah and Zalmunna said, 'Rise yourself and fall upon us, for as the man is, so is his strength.' And *Gideon arose and killed Zebah and Zalmunna.*"

The Spoils

Then Gideon "*took the crescent ornaments that were on the necks of their camels.*"

Some translations describe these ornaments as "little moons." They were crescent-shaped ornaments of either silver or gold that were worn around the necks of men, women, and camels. This practice continues today in parts of Arabia.

THINK AND GROW

In our modern era this scene is quite cruel, even barbaric. But Gideon was acting as God's Judge and carrying out the mission given to him by God.

Gideon has learned to trust God one step at a time – even when it is difficult.

Gideon was successful in his call because he was willing to allow God to use Him.

25

A Hero's Choice – 8:22-23

Then the men of Israel said to Gideon, "Rule over us, you and your son and your grandson also, for you have saved us from the hand of Midian."

Gideon said to them, "*I will not rule over you, and my son will not rule over you; the Lord will rule over you.*"

Judges 8:22-23

~ Note ~

In this passage there is an interesting question which I have not found the answer to. The suggestion is that Gideon, his son, *and his grandson* should rule over Israel. Gideon replies that neither he or his son will rule over them. The fact that Gideon does not say that his grandson will not rule over Israel makes me wonder if that was divinely left out. Could it be that one of the sons of Gideon's 70 sons did rule over Israel at a later date?

Decision Time

Gideon had become a national hero.

The temptation to accept the glory and honor of becoming their ruling monarch must have been great.

While not explicitly stated in this passage, it seems clear that Gideon was quick to seek the Lord in times of uncertainty or when he needed to make a decision.

Good Decision

His natural tendencies must have been very powerful with regard to being officially recognized by elevation to be Israel's king.

So how does Gideon respond to his nation wanting him to be elevated to King status?

"I will not rule over you, and my son will not rule over you; the Lord will rule over you."

Gideon was a devout servant of God and was not about to take the authority and glory that belonged exclusively to God.

In the New Testament we read that John the Baptist understood this important principle.

"You yourselves bear me witness, that I said, '*I am not the Christ*, but I have been sent before Him.' The one who has the bride is the bridegroom. The friend of the bridegroom, who stands and hears Him, rejoices greatly at the bridegroom's voice. Therefore this joy of mine is now complete. *He must increase, but I must decrease*'" (John 3:28-30).

The Apostle Paul stated this same truth: "Whether you eat or drink, or *whatever you do, do all to the glory of God*" (1 Corinthians 10:31-32).

After being an instrument of God to deliver Israel from its oppressors, Gideon refused the crown and glory offered by his grateful nation. He realized the victory and glory belonged exclusively to God – he made the right decision.

Gideon made the right decision by rejecting the offer of being Israel's king. He did not take any of the great power and resulting glory that belonged exclusively to God.

Parallelism

Gideon had accomplished his God-given call to deliver Israel from the neighboring terrorists of primarily Midianites but also bands of marauders from other surrounding nations. However, when asked to be king he refused.

In like manner Jesus had accomplished His God-given call and refused earthly kingship but instead was a servant.

"My kingdom is not of this world. If My kingdom were of this world, My servants would have been fighting, that I might not be delivered over to the Jews. But *My kingdom is not from the world"* (John 18:36).

Interesting

"The Lord said to Gideon, 'The people who are with you are too many for Me to give the Midianites into their hands, *lest Israel claim glory for itself* against Me, saying, *"My own hand has saved me"'"* (Judges 7:2).

Then in the next chapter we read: "The men of Israel said to Gideon, 'Rule over us, both you and your son, and your grandson also; for *you have delivered us* from the hand of Midian'" (Judges 8:22).

THINK AND GROW

~1~ How about you?

~~~a~ When you accomplish significant things in life, do you give God the glory?

~~~b~ When God uses you as a tool for accomplishing spiritual things, do you point to God?

~2~ Do you realize that you no longer belong to this world but rather you are a citizen of a far better country?

~3~ Do you stay conscious that you are just passing through this world and are headed to your homeland in heaven?

26

Spoils of War – 8:24-26

And Gideon said to them, "Let me make a request of you: every one of you *give me the earrings from his spoil.*" (For they had golden earrings, because they were Ishmaelites.) And they answered, "*We will willingly give them.*" And they spread a cloak, and every man threw in it the earrings of his spoil. And *the weight of the golden earrings that he requested was 1,700 shekels of gold*, besides the crescent ornaments and the pendants and the purple garments worn by the kings of Midian, and besides the collars that were around the necks of their camels.

Judges 8:24-26

Collect the Spoils

"And Gideon said to them, 'Let me make a request of you: every one of you *give me the earrings from his spoil.*' (For they had golden earrings, because they were Ishmaelites.)"

Motivation

Some scholars criticize Gideon at this point. However, as I read this passage, I find no hint as to what Gideon's motivation was:

- Did he want to avoid individual soldiers keeping war mementos?
- Did he want to use the wealth to help fund God's work?

- Did he have some nefarious goal in mind?

The Loot

"And they spread a cloak, and every man threw in it the earrings of his spoil. And *the weight of the golden earrings that he requested was 1,700 shekels of gold, besides the crescent ornaments and the pendants and the purple garments worn by the kings of Midian, and besides the collars that were around the necks of their camels.*"

What was the value of the spoils?

Gold shekels of that day are believed to have contained about four and a half grams of nearly pure gold. Some scholars have calculated the total gold to be more than forty-two pounds. In early 2024 an ounce of gold was worth about US$2,100 making the total value of just the gold loot to be about one and a half million U.S. dollars. In terms of ancient prices, that would have been a huge amount. Add in all the other loot and they got quite a haul.

A Hero of the Faith

One thing we do know is that Gideon is a "hero of the faith" according to the Hall of Faith chapter in the New Testament:

"Now faith is the assurance of things hoped for, the conviction of things not seen. For by it the people of old received their commendation... And what more shall I say? For time would fail me to tell of *Gideon*, Barak, Samson, Jephthah, of David and Samuel and the prophets—who through faith conquered kingdoms, enforced justice, obtained promises, stopped the mouths of lions, quenched the power of fire, escaped the edge of the sword, were made strong out of weakness, became mighty in war, put foreign armies to flight" (Hebrews 11:1-2, 32-34).

THINK AND GROW

We have followed Gideon from a doubter who was raised up by God for a specific purpose. As his faith grew God used him in a mighty way, so much so that he became a hero to Israel and an example to us – identified as such in the New Testament.

Gideon's story illustrates how God uses ordinary people as tools to accomplish His plans. The key to spiritual success is faith and a willingness, followed by obedience. He was willing to go against the flow and take unpopular stands.

God can and will accomplish His purposes through anyone, even those who are timid and initially lack faith. Spiritual leaders are rarely those who are bold and extroverted.

Weakness and lack of ability is never an adequate excuse for not obeying God. Weak, prone to sin, earthen vessels like you and me bring glory to God when we allow God to use us.

God is sovereign and always sees far more than we do.

If you are willing to grow spiritually, God wants to use you. He wants to do great things through you. God never relies on human strength, rather He provides His strength working through you.

We have tremendous advantages Gideon lacked. First, the Spirit of God continuously lives within each and every believer. He is always with you, willing to provide guidance and confidence. Second, we have the written Word of God readily available to us at all times.

~1~ God often uses tough times to get our attention.

~~~a~ Have you ever experienced this?

~~~b~ Are you experiencing a tough period in your life now?

~~~c~ In tough times in the future will you commit to see them as a grace gift from God?

~2~ Have you ignored God when He spoke to you in the past?

~~~a~ If so, what were your excuses for not following His requests?

~~~b~ Are you willing to commit to obedience in the future?

~3~ Like Gideon you can push beyond your doubts and fears.

~~~a~ Remind yourself of all that God has done for you in your past.

~~~b~ Trust that God is with you all the way.

~~~c~ Give God the recognition and glory He deserves for each and every accomplishment He provides.

~4~ Do you sense God speaking to you now?

~~~a~ Do you truly believe that God wants to do great things through you?

~~~b~ Are some of your thoughts quite different than God's thoughts?

~~~c~ Is there something which comes to your mind now, that you know you should trust Him to accomplish through you?
~~~

27

Gideon's Ephod – 8:24-27

And Gideon said to them, "Let me make a request of you: every one of you give me the earrings from his spoil." (For they had golden earrings, because they were Ishmaelites.) And they answered, "We will willingly give them." And they spread a cloak, and every man threw in it the earrings of his spoil. And the weight of the golden earrings that he requested was 1,700 shekels of gold, besides the crescent ornaments and the pendants and the purple garments worn by the kings of Midian, and besides the collars that were around the necks of their camels.

And Gideon made an ephod of it and put it in his city, in Ophrah. And *all Israel whored after it there, and it became a snare to Gideon and to his family.*

Judges 8:24-27

Following significant spiritual victories is often a time of significant spiritual failure. There are a number of such examples throughout Scripture.

Ephod

Originally an ephod was a sacred item that was worn by the high priest. We read about the priest's garments: "Bring near to you Aaron your brother, and his sons with him, from among the people of Israel, to serve Me as priests—Aaron and Aaron's sons, Nadab and Abihu, Eleazar and Ithamar... These are the garments that they shall make: a breastpiece, *an ephod*, a robe, a coat of checker work, a turban, and a sash... And *they shall make the ephod of gold, of blue and purple and scarlet yarns, and of fine twined linen, skillfully worked*" (Exodus 28:1, 4, 6).

The ephod included a breastplate attached by gold chains and cords which were tied to gold rings. All of this included lots of gold and twelve precious stones making it very valuable.

The ephod was a vehicle for obtaining instructions from God.

Later ephods were worn by ordinary priests: "Then the king said to Doeg, 'You turn and strike the priests.' And Doeg the Edomite turned and struck down the priests, and he killed on that day eighty-five persons *who wore the linen ephod*" (1 Samuel 22:18).

~ Note ~

Since ephods were to be worn and there is no mention of Gideon or anyone else wearing his ephod, some scholars believe this was not the typical ephod made as clothing but rather a purposeful trophy or monument.

Motivation

Gideon had rebuked his people for proposing he become king in recognition of *his victory* when he understood that *victory belongs to God*. Therefore, their adoration should be to God alone.

What was the motivation Gideon had for making an ephod? Scripture does not tell us, but it may well have been to make a sacred memorial commemorating the victory God had provided, and to obtain further directions from God.

As emphasis it would likely have all the tribe names inscribed on it as a collective statement that they were all God's victorious people. (All the tribes had contributed their spoils.) I believe Gideon's motivation in making this ephod was righteous – a means of giving credit to God.

Considering the overall context this is the likely purpose. Gideon was making an ephod as a testimonial to God. It was probably a direct response to their request for him to become their king. The people had given him the credit for victory – rather than to God. Gideon responded that neither he nor one of his sons would ever rule over them.

Instead, an ephod would be made to help lead his people in the worship of God. It would be a tool for praise and worship of God. I believe Gideon wanted to do this as a testimonial for all Israel to recognize that it is only God to be worshipped and to rule over them.

~ Notes ~

[1] Some see a parallel here to when Moses was meeting with God and *the people made a golden calf.* I do not see this, since the passage clearly says, "*Gideon* made an ephod."

[2] Many scholars, including some that I have very high respect for, believe Gideon's making of an ephod was wrong. I do not find any direct Biblical evidence of that – unless you jump ahead and see how it became an idol at a later time.

Ophrah

"*And Gideon made an ephod* of it and *put it in his city, in Ophrah.*"

Ophrah is believed to be about five miles east of Bethel.

The gender-neutral name Ophrah means *young deer* or *fawn*.

Significance

The reality of this significant event is that we find that once again God's chosen people do not trust Him or give Him due credit and glory. They become apostate and break His clear commandment to not make or worship idols. Their historical cycle of apostasy continues.

Wrong Application

"And *all Israel whored after it there, and it became a snare to Gideon and to his family.*"

Regardless of Gideon's purpose for creating the ephod, it did not take long for the Israelites to begin worshipping it! As a result "*it became a snare to Gideon and to his family.*" This may indicate that his family had reversed their worship back to idol worship.

Nowhere does it indicate that Gideon worshipped his ephod as an idol.

But what exactly does "*became a snare*" mean? Possibly this indicates remorse because of the fact he had built the ephod. Maybe he had remorse since there is no indication that he sought God about building it beforehand.

THINK AND GROW

~1~ What do you think the meaning of the ephod becoming a snare is?

Gideon apparently made the ephod as a way of remembering God's victory on their behalf.

~2~ Do you have any deliberate way of remembering past spiritual events (such as a journal or other written form)? If not, do think it would be good to initiate one?

28

40 Years – 8:28

So Midian was subdued before the people of Israel, and *they raised their heads no more.*

And *the land had rest forty years in the days of Gideon.*

Judges 8:28

As a result of Gideon's emphatic victory, the Midianites and other surrounding marauders were fearful of Gideon and his troops. Peace came to Israel and they enjoyed peace with their neighbors with Gideon serving as Judge. It was a spiritually rewarding time as Israel once again worshipped the one true God. This peace lasted for forty years.

Head Position

"They raised their heads no more."

Now with their attacking enemies subdued by the Israelites, they were no longer in constant fear of imminent danger.

Because of their victories, they did not need to be constantly searching the horizon for new bands of invaders. While they must constantly be alert, the extreme urgency of vigilance had been greatly reduced.

Recall that when God told Gideon to reduce the size of his army, one of the tests was whether the potential soldiers drank water from their cupped hands or lapped the water with their tongues. This may have been because those who drank from their hands could more easily raise their heads to scan the horizon for approaching enemies.

~ Note ~

Some scholars offer an alternative view of this phrase. This phrase could be in reference to the Midianites who have been subdued and therefore have no need to keep raising their heads as they observe ways to attack Israel.

Rest

"The land had rest forty years in the days of Gideon."

There was a time of peace. No invading marauders, no destruction of crops, no pillaging, no wars.

Forty years is about the length of a generation.

~ Note ~

The typical ending for each of the judges that is recorded in the Book of Judges was a period of peace.

This, however, is the last time in the book that we find a prolonged period of peace.

Bookends

"Forty years of rest" are like bookends to the story of Gideon.

At the beginning of the historical account of Gideon we read:

> "And *the land had rest for forty years.* The people of Israel did what was evil in the sight of the Lord, and the Lord gave them into the hand of Midian seven years. And the hand of Midian overpowered Israel, and because of Midian the people of Israel made for themselves the dens that are in the mountains and the caves and the strongholds" (Judges 5:31-6:2).

The account of Gideon's life is contained in Chapters 6-8 of the Book of Judges. Just prior to Gideon's death we read once again of a quiet period in Israel's history.

> "So Midian was subdued before the people of Israel, and they raised their heads no more. And *the land had rest forty years* in the days of Gideon" (Judges 8:28).

THINK AND GROW

"Midian was subdued before the people of Israel" is an example of an important principle: If we are to have peace, we must subdue our spiritual enemies.

As Christians we are admonished to always be on the alert (but not in a state of panic).

"Humble yourselves, therefore, under the mighty hand of God so that at the proper time He may exalt you, casting all your anxieties on Him, because He cares for you. Be sober-minded; *be watchful.* Your adversary the devil prowls around like a roaring lion, seeking someone to devour. Resist him, firm in your faith, knowing that the same kinds of suffering are being experienced by your brotherhood throughout the world. And after you have suffered a little while, the God of all grace, Who has called you to His eternal glory in Christ, will Himself restore, confirm, strengthen, and establish you. To Him be the dominion forever and ever. Amen" (1 Peter 5:6-11).

"*You keep him in perfect peace whose mind is stayed on You*, because he trusts in You. Trust in the Lord forever, for the Lord God is an everlasting Rock" (Isaiah 26:3-4).

"Rejoice in the Lord always; again I will say, Rejoice. Let your reasonableness be known to everyone. The Lord is at hand; *do not be anxious about anything*, but in everything by prayer and supplication with thanksgiving let your requests be made known to God. And *the peace of God, which surpasses all understanding, will guard your hearts and your minds in Christ Jesus*" (Philippians 4:4-7).

"Put on then, as God's chosen ones, holy and beloved, compassion, kindness, humility, meekness, and patience, bearing with one another and, if one has a complaint against another, forgiving each other; as the Lord has forgiven you, so you also must forgive. And above all these put on love, which binds everything together in perfect harmony. And *let the peace of Christ rule in your hearts*, to which indeed you were called in one body. And be thankful. Let the Word of Christ dwell in you richly, teaching and admonishing one another in all wisdom, singing psalms and hymns and spiritual songs, with thankfulness in your hearts to God. And whatever you do, in word or deed, do everything in the name of the Lord Jesus, giving thanks to God the Father through Him" (Colossians 3:12-17).

29

Gideon's Death – 8:29-32

Jerubbaal the son of Joash went and lived in his own house. Now *Gideon had seventy sons*, his own offspring, for *he had many wives*. And *his concubine who was in Shechem also bore him a son*, and he called his name Abimelech. And *Gideon the son of Joash died in a good old age* and was buried in the tomb of Joash his father, at Ophrah of the Abiezrites.

Judges 8:29-32

Two Names

This passage begins with Jerubbaal and then once again uses the name Gideon. Perhaps this is to remind us of his earlier defeat of Baal: "Therefore on that day Gideon was called Jerubbaal, that is to say, 'Let Baal contend against him,' because he broke down his altar" (Judges 6:32).

Wives and Sons

We find this conquering hero of Israel now settles down with many wives – who gave him 70 sons (and an unknown number of daughters).

He also had a relationship with a concubine in the town of Shechem who bore another son, Abimelech. This was a disobedient act against God's law for His chosen people.

'When the Lord your God brings you into the land that you are entering to take possession of it, and clears away many nations before you, the Hittites, the Girgashites, the Amorites, the Canaanites, the Perizzites, the Hivites, and the Jebusites, seven nations more numerous and mightier than yourselves, and when the Lord your God gives them over to you, and you defeat them, then you must devote them to complete destruction. *You shall make no covenant with them* and show no mercy to them. *You shall not intermarry with them*, giving your daughters to their sons or taking their daughters for your sons, for they would turn away your sons from following me, to serve other gods. Then the anger of the Lord would be kindled against you, and he would destroy you quickly. But thus shall you deal with them: you shall break down their altars and dash in pieces their pillars and chop down their Asherim and burn their carved images with fire" (Deuteronomy 7:1-5).

Abimelech

Of the seventy sons, only Abimelech is mentioned by name. Unfortunately, Abimelech ushers in a sad new era of Israel's history which we read about in the next chapter in the Book of Judges (Judges 9).

It is interesting to note that the name Abimelech means "my father is king."

Abimelech rebelled and lived an evil, tragic life. He murdered all his half-brothers and died in battle after a short reign.

Words vs. Actions

Gideon had previously said he would not be king, but he ended up acting like a king.

"Gideon said to them, '*I will not rule over you*, nor shall my son rule over you; the Lord shall rule over you'" (Judges 8:23).

"*Gideon had seventy sons*, his own offspring, for *he had many wives*. And *his concubine who was in Shechem also bore him a son*, and he called his name Abimelech" (Judges 8:30-31).

Old Age

Like many Old Testament individuals Gideon lived a long life.

~ Note ~

Some scholars liken Gideon to Samson in that they both died in disgrace. In Gideon's case it was for having taken retribution on Succoth and Penuel for their lack of assistance in the war effort. Also, they believe he behaved badly by making the ephod – which resulted in the people reverting to worshipping a false god.

One preacher for whom I have a lot of respect put it this way: "Gideon came from humble origins, but God chose him to lead the children of Israel into battle. God used him mightily to vanquish Israel's enemies. But in the end, Gideon lowered his standards, and he fell into immorality and pride. His beginnings were good. He had his great moments. But everything came crashing down in the end." —Greg Laurie

One thing we do know is that Gideon was a sinner just like all the rest of us – but God used him mightily.

Tomb

Gideon was *"buried in the tomb of Joash his father, at Ophrah of the Abiezrites."*

Joash was buried in the City of David (in Jerusalem) rather than in the tombs of the kings (2 Chronicles 24:25; 2 Kings 12:21).

~ Notes ~

[1] The City of David (Wadi Hilweh) can be visited today where archaeological digs have uncovered much of the area that dates to the Bronze and Iron Ages.

[2] The Book of Judges contains more information about Gideon than any other Judge.

THINK AND GROW

The Christian life is a life-long battle against our sin nature. We constantly battle (1) our flesh, (2) our eyes, and (3) pride.

"Do not love the world or the things in the world. If anyone loves the world, the love of the Father is not in him. For all that is in the world—*the desires of the flesh* and *the desires of the eyes* and *pride in possessions*—is not from the Father but is from the world. And the world is passing away along with its desires, but whoever does the will of God abides forever" (1 John 2:15-17).

~ Important Warning ~

As we become spiritually stronger, we become a greater target for Satan. This is because when we are not effective for God, Satan has no reason to knock us down.

After living a largely spiritually strong life, Gideon fell by taking a foreign concubine and fathered a son who lived an evil life.

~1~ If you died today, what spiritual legacy would you leave? (1—10)

~2~ Consider some of the tools you have to leave a strong legacy.

~~~a~ Are you regularly in the Word of God?

"For the Word of God is living and active, sharper than any two-edged sword, piercing to the division of soul and of spirit, of joints and of marrow, and discerning the thoughts and intentions of the heart" (Hebrews 4:12).

~~~b~ Do you rely on the Holy Spirit Who indwells you to guide and protect you?

Just prior to returning to heaven Jesus said, "When the Spirit of truth comes, He will guide you into all the truth, for He will not speak on His own authority, but whatever He hears He will speak, and He will declare to you the things that are to come. He will glorify Me, for he will take what is mine and declare it to you" (John 16:13-14).

~~~c~ Are you in constant communion with God?

"When He comes on that day to be glorified in His saints, and to be marveled at among all who have believed, because our testimony to you was believed. *To this end we always pray for you, that our God may make you worthy of His calling* and may fulfill every resolve for good and every work of faith *by His power*" (2 Thessalonians 1:10-12).

~~~d~ Do you maintain a clear and constant focus on God's will for you?

"At the end of that time, *I, Nebuchadnezzar, raised my eyes toward heaven, and my sanity was restored...* At the same time that *my sanity was restored*, my honor and splendor were returned to me for the glory of my kingdom. My advisers and nobles sought me out, and I was restored to my throne and became even greater than before" (Daniel 4:34a, 36 niv).

~~~e~ Are you willing and committed to obey even when you don't understand?

The Apostle Paul wrote: "Not that I have already obtained this or am already perfect, but *I press on* to make it my own, because Christ Jesus has made me His own. Brothers, I do not consider that I have made it my own. But *one thing I do: forgetting what lies behind and straining forward to what lies ahead, I press on toward the goal* for the prize of the upward call of God in Christ Jesus. *Let those of us who are mature think this way*" (Philippians 3:12-15a).
~~~

30

Apostasy Returns – 8:33-35

As soon as Gideon died, the people of Israel turned again and whored after the Baals and made Baal-berith their god. And the people of Israel did not remember the Lord their God, who had delivered them from the hand of all their enemies on every side, and they did not show steadfast love to the family of Jerubbaal (that is, Gideon) in return for all the good that he had done to Israel.

Judges 8:33-35

Leadership

"As soon as Gideon died, the people of Israel turned again and whored after the Baals."

God often chooses His leaders in unusual ways. No one in Israel would have suspected that timid, shy, scared Gideon would lead their nation to victory even though vastly outnumbered. Or that forty years of peace were on the horizon due to God working through this farm boy.

Good leadership at the top is always important. Leader Gideon dies and the nation quickly falls back into its prior sinful ways.

Forty years of prosperous times under Judge Gideon reverted at his death to the Canaanite way of life.

Baal-Berith

"As soon as Gideon died, the people of Israel turned again and whored after the Baals and *made Baal-berith their god.*"

Baal-berith means "*Baal of the Covenant.*" In fact, later this false god is referred to as "El-berith" (Judges 9:46). This is an example of Satan's typical evil substitution for reality, in this case the covenant relationship God had with Israel.

The Semantic title "El-*name*" referred to any of many different gods. When simply labeled "El" it referred to "The God."

Short Memory

The people of Israel *did not remember the Lord their God*, who had delivered them."

Now we find the Israelites worshipping the memorial (ephod) which Gideon had made – they attributed their successes to Baal-Berith ("*Baal of the Covenant*") instead of to God.

Lack of Appreciation

"*They did not show steadfast love to the family of Jerubbaal (that is, Gideon) in return for all the good that he had done to Israel.*"

Being on top doesn't typically last long, and that is still true today. This has been expressed in our era by the somewhat familiar slogan, "What have you done for me today?"

The Conclusion

Prosperity and good times often bring complacency.

After all the victories and success God had given Israel to get them out of their turbulent times, we find that pleasant times can easily allow complacence and sliding back into prior bad habits.

THINK AND GROW

Gideon's story is not unlike our stories today. It is in the tough times we typically experience the most spiritual growth.

It is our reliance on God, our humility, and our obedient faithfulness that largely determine our usefulness to God.

It is only by obedience to God that we can be sure of winning.

Gideon's example reveals that we need to get our personal lives right. Only then can we truly be what God wants us to be in our public life.

~ Note ~

Throughout Scripture the pattern is constant. God uses individuals as opposed to teams or committees. While it is true that individuals often team up together, individuals should be right with God in order to be useful in the team or committee.

~1~ It is easy to fall away from God. Have you experienced that?

~2~ Has there been a time when you were proud of what you had done for God?

~3~ Do you recall a tough time in your life which resulted in strong spiritual growth?

CONCLUSIONS

195

31

Recap – Philippians 4:19

And my God will supply every need of yours according to His riches
in glory in Christ Jesus.

Philippians 4:19

At the beginning of the account of Gideon's life we find Israel in a state of apostasy and suffering at the hands of oppressors.

In the middle of the account, we find God raises up an unlikely hero to lead His people and to gain victory against overwhelming odds. Gideon was a doubter and reluctant to trust God, but he overcame his doubt and became obedient to the work that God had called him to do.

At the end of the account, the Israelites are once again in a state of apostasy and headed into more tough times.

Pattern of Progress

~ Least Likely to Succeed ~

"And he said to Him, 'Please, Lord, how can I save Israel? Behold, my clan is the weakest in Manasseh, and I am the least in my father's house" (Judges 6:15).

~ Obedient ~

"Gideon took ten men of his servants and did as the Lord had told him" (Judges 6:27a).

~ Seeks Confirmation ~

"Then Gideon said to God, 'If you will save Israel by my hand, as You have said, behold, I am laying a fleece of wool on the threshing floor. If there is dew on the fleece alone, and it is dry on all the ground, then I shall know that You will save Israel by my hand, as You have said.' And it was so. When he rose early next morning and squeezed the fleece, he wrung enough dew from the fleece to fill a bowl with water. Then Gideon said to God, 'Let not Your anger burn against me; let me speak just once more. Please let me test just once more with the fleece. Please let it be dry on the fleece only, and on all the ground let there be dew.' And God did so that night; and it was dry on the fleece only, and on all the ground there was dew" (Judges 6:36-40).

~ Worshipping ~

"As soon as Gideon heard the telling of the dream and its interpretation, he worshiped" (Judges 7:13a).

~ Victorious ~

"Every man stood in his place around the camp, and all the army ran. They cried out and fled. When they blew the 300 trumpets, the Lord set every man's sword against his comrade and against all the army. And the army fled as far as Beth-shittah toward Zererah, as far as the border of Abel-meholah, by Tabbath" (Judges 7:21-22).

~ Proper Perspective ~

"Then the men of Israel said to Gideon, 'Rule over us, you and your son and your grandson also, for you have saved us from the hand of

Midian.' Gideon said to them, 'I will not rule over you, and my son will not rule over you; the Lord will rule over you'" (Judges 8:22-23).

~ Peace Through Strength ~

"And the land had rest forty years in the days of Gideon" (Judges 8:28b).

Additional Gideon Scripture

~ Isaiah 9 ~

"But there'll be no darkness for those who were in trouble. Earlier He did bring the lands of Zebulun and Naphtali into disrepute, but the time is coming when He'll make that whole area glorious—the road along the Sea, the country past the Jordan, international Galilee. The people who walked in darkness have seen a great light. For those who lived in a land of deep shadows—light! Sunbursts of light! You repopulated the nation, You expanded its joy. Oh, they're so glad in Your presence! Festival joy! The joy of a great celebration, sharing rich gifts and warm greetings.

"The abuse of oppressors and cruelty of tyrants — all their whips and cudgels and curses — is gone, done away with, *a deliverance as surprising and sudden as Gideon's old victory over Midian.*

"The boots of all those invading troops, along with their shirts soaked with innocent blood, will be piled in a heap and burned, a fire that will burn for days! *For a Child has been born — for us! The gift of a Son — for us! He'll take over the running of the world. His names will be: Amazing Counselor, Strong God, Eternal Father, Prince of Wholeness.*

"His ruling authority will grow, and there'll be no limits to the wholeness He brings. He'll rule from the historic David throne over that promised kingdom. He'll put that kingdom on a firm footing and keep it going with fair dealing and right living, beginning now and lasting always. The zeal of God-of-the-Angel-Armies will do all this" (Isaiah 9:1-7 msg).

~ Hebrews 11 ~

"Now faith is the substance of things hoped for, the evidence of things not seen. For by it the elders obtained a good testimony. By faith we understand that the worlds were framed by the Word of God, so that the things which are seen were not made of things which are visible...

"And what more shall I say? For the time would fail me to tell of *Gideon* and Barak and Samson and Jephthah, also of David and Samuel and the prophets: who through faith subdued kingdoms, worked righteousness, obtained promises, stopped the mouths of lions, quenched the violence of fire, escaped the edge of the sword, out of weakness were made strong, became valiant in battle, turned to flight the armies of the aliens" (Hebrews 11:1-3, 32-34).

THINK AND GROW

Not much has changed about human nature and abilities since the days of Gideon. When we have faith and put our trust in God, He can turn our weakness into strength.

~1~ Do you believe, that like Gideon, God *could* do great things through you if you are willing and obedient?

"Only he who believes is obedient. Only he who is obedient believes." —Dietrich Bonhoffer

~2~ Do you believe that God *wants* to use you?

32

Final Thoughts – Proverbs 3:5-7

Trust in the Lord with all your heart, and do not lean on your own understanding. In all your ways acknowledge Him, and He will make straight your paths. Be not wise in your own eyes; fear the Lord, and turn away from evil.

Proverbs 3:5-7

Throughout this book we have observed many take-away lessons. In this final chapter we consider some over-arching themes.

- The spiritual battle we face is not ours, but God's.

- Doubts do not disqualify you from faith.

- Put your trust in Him, depend on Him, and He will give you direction.

- God's faithfulness toward you in the past is a call to your ongoing faith in the future.

- God wants His children to face life and its battles with confidence through faith in Him.

- Gideon should be an encouragement to all of us – God can use anyone, including you and me, to accomplish His purposes.

- God sees our potential and what we could become, not the way we are today.

- Our private devotion and faithfulness are a priority before God uses us. Put your private life in order – there are no shortcuts.

- As God gives us success, we must remember that it came from Him.

- As God gives us success, we should regularly recount the victory.

- God is a God of second (and third...) chances. Your past failures are irrelevant to what God can and will do for you now and in the future – absolutely nothing disqualifies you from future usefulness in God's work.

- Be careful of excessive rest. Past victories can lead to complacency which often leads to spiritual failure.

Quotes

"God is looking for people through whom he can do the impossible – what a pity that we plan only the things that we can do by ourselves." —A.W. Tozer

"The world has yet to see what God can do with a man fully consecrated to him." —D.L. Moody

THINK AND GROW

Having your private life right with God is a prerequisite for public usefulness. Often being fully devoted to God and His direction can be personally costly.

~1~ Are there areas in your life that you need to confess to Jesus Christ?

~2~ Are there any idols in your life which you need to separate from?

~3~ Are you willing to give up whatever is required to be fully dedicated to God?

I Am a Gideon

December 3, 2018 ~ Made of Still

Faith and Motivation ~ Heather Chesiyna

*And he said unto him, Oh my Lord, wherewith shall I save Israel?
Behold, my family is poor in Manasseh, and I am the least in my father's
house. And the Lord said unto him, Surely I will be with thee, and thou
shalt smite the Midianites as one man.* —Judges 6:15-16

When I was in high school, we had a Christian Union comprised of 12 women of God. Every year, they prayed and fasted to select Bible study leaders. I found it strange that they would take the act of choosing Bible study leaders seriously to the point of fasting. One day during our meetings, I felt something in my spirit... a calling. I wanted to run. The Christian Union announced the 2003 Bible Study Leaders, they stated that the person you will be named after would be a recurring theme in your life. Then one of the members announced, "The Bible study leader for Bible Study Gideon is...." Alas, it was me. I was 16 years old at this time, and I started studying Judges 6-8. I first wanted to understand who Gideon was. Every week, I would prepare a sermon and study material for my group. As it turns out, as I grew older and wiser and full of faith, Gideon indeed became a recurring theme in my life.

Gideon is a man that everyone needs to know. He was the least in absolutely everything. I believe he felt insignificant and outnumbered by fellow people in his time. At this low point in his life, an angel appeared and declared something opposite of his circumstance. The angel declared him a MIGHTY MAN OF VALOR. Isn't it beautiful that God sees you at that point of completion and that point of victory? He sees past you're here and now. It reminds me of Moses who had a stammering tongue but still, God chose him to speak on behalf of God and Israel. See, if we let God, he will take our weakness and use it. His strength is made perfect through our weakness.

The story of Gideon must be told currently. *Today's world embraces perfection, or should I say the thought of perfection.* If you must be a public speaker, you must be eloquent and have an arsenal of vocabulary at the back of your mind. If you want to be a model, you can't have an ounce of fat to your body. There seems to be *little room for a margin of error in today's world.* The world defines perfection, and man agrees to the unachievable standard.

The story of Gideon must be told because it shows that God has selected you, with that chip on the shoulder. You who has a limp and insecurities. He sees beyond your flaws and sees you as a vessel; your task is only to yield to him. We need to understand that weaknesses are a platform for God to demonstrate His strength and glory. He wants to multiply you because you will know without a shadow of a doubt that you did not do it with your power.

I have been in many situations that the odds were not in my favor. Still, I yielded to God when it made no sense. That act of faith always transcends in the spirit realm, and things shift. Then alas, I repeatedly confess in awe, THAT WAS AN ACT OF GOD.

I believe we all have a part of Gideon in us. A part of our lives that we see as insignificant. Still, God says, I want you. Trust and believe that God wants to use you. Don't throw in the towel, what God has in store might surprise you!

Appendix B – Mt. 28:18-20
The Gideons International

Jesus's direction to His followers:

All authority in heaven and on earth has been given to Me. *Go therefore and make disciples of all nations*, baptizing them in the name of the Father and of the Son and of the Holy Spirit, teaching them to observe all that I have commanded you. And behold, *I am with you always, to the end of the age.*

Matthew 28:18-20

Many people, Christians and non-Christians alike, are at least somewhat familiar with *The Gideons International* organization. They are best known for placing Bibles in hotels around the world.

They also place Bibles and New Testaments in many other locations around the world including but not limited to, hotels, motels, bed and breakfasts, jails and prisons, military, middle schools, high schools, colleges and universities, hospitals and medical offices, first responders, legal offices, as well to individuals in the midst of suffering from natural disasters.

The organization was founded by two traveling businessmen in 1898, and began distributing Scripture into the traffic lanes of life a decade later. As I write this, *The Gideons* are distributing more than two copies every second 24/7/365 and they have distributed a total in excess of 2.5 *billion* copies of Scripture to date.

~ Anecdote ~

My wife and I joined *The Gideons* in early 2005. We have both been privileged to serve in a number of ways in the years since. I highly recommend *Gideon* membership to any Bible believing Christian.

Core Message

The one and only purpose of *The Gideons* is to help individuals come to a saving knowledge of Jesus Christ, to have a personal relationship with Him including an eternal life of joy in heaven.

GPS

One of my favorite ways to explain salvation is **"God's GPS"**

- The *Best and Most Important* GPS you will ever obtain
- It requires *no software* updates
- It doesn't even need any *batteries*
- It will take you to *the very best of all destinations*
- It will *correct you when you get off course*
- *God's **Plan** of **Salvation*** as found in the Holy Bible

THINK AND GROW

~1~ How about you? Are you a born-again child of God?

~2~ If you are, why not become a *Gideon*?

https://www.gideons.org/

About the Author

Robert Lloyd Russell

Biography

Robert Lloyd Russell's books have won national and international literary awards including a World Book Award (one of just three awards across all genres). He is the editor of a book containing transcribed spoken messages of martyred missionary Jim Elliot. As a small boy Robert lived in the Elliot home at a time prior to Jim's departure for the mission field. The transcriptions were carefully made from old wire recordings, the forerunner of magnetic tape recordings. Jim was one of Robert's Sunday School teachers and Jim's father was one of his spiritual mentors.

Russell has a diverse secular background which spans many functions including engineering, manufacturing, sales, marketing, and staff positions. His technical career included the management of a wide variety of engineers, physicists, and scientists in the high-technology industry.

During the 1970s while he was Camera Engineering Manager for a Fortune 500 corporation, he became fascinated with the attributes of light and the parallels to the attributes of God. He would later write about these parallels in some of his books.

In the early 1970s a senior executive of a major corporation began seeking Robert's opinions and advice. This was the start of a part-time consulting business. Then, from 1990 until his retirement in 2005, Robert devoted his entire career to advising and coaching many executives in a variety of organizations. Based in Portland, Oregon, his consulting practice routinely provided coaching and counseling on a wide range of business issues including ethics, overall effectiveness and profitability, organizational cultural issues, and Total Quality concepts.

During the 1980s as an active Christian businessman concerned about ethics, Robert enrolled in seminary and earned a Master of Christian Leadership degree from Western Seminary. For many years he was a popular adult Sunday School and Bible Study teacher.

Robert refers to himself as a simple **A-B-C** kind of guy: Christian **A**uthor, Christian **B**logger, and Christian **C**onsultant and **C**oach. His blog entitled "Abundant Life Now[1]" has been read in nearly 200 countries and translated into more than 100 languages.

---

1. http://robertlloydrussell.blogspot.com/

Want Free Books?

As an author, I want to thank you for reading this book and I regard the feedback of my readers very highly.

When considering buying a book many people weigh reviews carefully before deciding to purchase. If you enjoyed this book, would you consider assisting me by helping others make an informed decision? Leaving a review (even just a star rating without commentary) can help spread the message of the Gospel and increase others' faith through these books. It is also a great way to support this international ministry.

Robert Lloyd Russell's Newsletter[1]

Sign up for occasional updates from author Robert Lloyd Russell: https://www.subscribepage.com/rlr

He is committed to not bothering you with frequent newsletters. When he does send out occasional communications, it will contain one or more of the following:

- Advance information about current projects
- Related news
- Prayer requests
- Notification of **FREE eBooks** for a limited time
- Other items which may be of interest

(If you decide you no longer want to receive the newsletter, you may take advantage of the "unsubscribe" option at the bottom of each email.)

---

1. *https://www.subscribepage.com/rlr*

|||||

Robert Lloyd Russell's eBooks are available from your favorite online eBook retailer.

You may also want to visit the author's book website Books by Robert Lloyd Russell that lists his eBooks and printed books along with additional information, (booksrlr), or go to Books to Read[2] (https://books2read.com/ap/81Ym5B/Robert-Lloyd-Russell).

|||||

You are invited to connect with Robert Lloyd Russell through his daily internet blog *Abundant Life Now*[3] for inspiration and insight. (http://robertlloydrussell.blogspot.com/)

---

2. https://books2read.com/ap/81Ym5B/Robert-Lloyd-Russell

3. *http://RobertLloydRussell.blogspot.com/*

What To Read Next

eBook ISBN: 978-1393359371 ASIN: B083L97PZV ~ Print ISBN: 979-8223228738

An easy-to-read devotional style book which presents new and unforgettable insights. This landmark book identifies fascinating parallels between natural and spiritual light. Analogies teach profound truth in simple language.

"First there was Tozer with *The Knowledge of the Holy,* and then Packer gave us *Knowing God,* and now Russell has taken us further." —Dr. Earl D. Radmacher, General Editor, Nelson Study Bible/New King James Study Bible

Note: This eBook is an update of the first two sections of an earlier print book *GOD LIGHT: Sunlight Sonlight,* which **won six awards.**

Choose your favorite retailer (available in eBook or print: about 206 pages)

https://books2read.com/GodsNature

eBook ISBN: 978-1393518266 ASIN: B0874CHLD7 ~ Print ISBN: 979-8215346204

Dr. Ronald B. Allen, a nationally recognized expert on the Psalms, described this book as "The definitive work on Psalm 1."

A timely book for those who long for faster, more consistent spiritual growth. In today's Christian communities many are complacent in their ultimate destination and they neglect the importance of the journey. In so doing, they miss out on many of the here and now benefits of their adoption into the family of God. The normal (not average) Christian is growing more like Jesus Christ as they continue their life on earth. If you long to be a disciple who pleases God, this book is for you. This book is extremely relevant to today's culture.

Choose your favorite retailer (available in eBook or print: about 172 pages)

https://books2read.com/GodsChild

eBook ISBN: 978-1393268093 ASIN: B07XFPMVQT ~ Print ISBN: 978-1393348597

Early in the book the author provides a straightforward look at the three most popular interpretations of the parable of the pearl of great price. Included is a clear Bible-based rejection of the common notion that the pearl represents salvation. The major portion of the work provides parallels between the "one pearl of great price" and the Christian Church. Presented are seven unique aspects of a pearl which parallel the uniqueness of the Church. Finally, eight additional characteristics of a pearl and their parallels are presented.

Note: This eBook is an update of an earlier print book *ONE PRECIOUS PEARL: God's Design for His Church*, which **won five awards**.

Choose your favorite retailer (available in eBook or print: about 140 pages)

https://books2read.com/GodsChurch

eBook ISBN: 978-1393844402 ASIN: B091XZF79B ~ Print ISBN: 979-8223262800

Written for those who long for faster, more consistent spiritual growth. Many in today's Christian communities are complacent about their ultimate destination and they neglect the importance of the journey. In so doing, they miss out on many of the here and now benefits of their adoption into the family of God. The normal (not average) Christian is growing more like Jesus Christ as they continue their life on earth. If you long to be a disciple who pleases God, this book is for you.

Choose your favorite retailer (available in eBook or Print: about 152 pages).

https://books2read.com/ChristsDisciple

eBook ISBN: 978-1393211785 ASIN: B08H4F619W ~ Print ISBN: 979-8223962915

This book develops two graphic models. The "Christian Life Model" is about victorious Christian living. Included in this section are the author's detailed acrostics for fellowship, obedience, power, prayer, witness, and the Word.

The "Christian Guidance Model" shows the interrelationship of the "Christian Life Model" and one's inner convictions, Godly counsel, and the Lordship of Jesus Christ.

Note: This eBook is an update of an earlier print book "*THY WILL BE DONE ON EARTH: Understanding God's Will for You.*"

Choose your favorite retailer (available in eBook or print: about 204 pages)

https://books2read.com/GodsDesire

eBook ISBN: 978-1393424994 ~ Print ISBN: 979-8223726906

An easy-to-read devotional style book which identifies parallels between the reactions of physical objects to natural light and the reactions of humans to spiritual light. These analogies teach profound truth in simple language.

Written in short easily digestible segments, it is ideal reading for the person on the go. Readers gain a greater appreciation regarding Christians shining like lights.

Note: This eBook is an update of the third section of an earlier print book *GOD LIGHT: Sonlight Sunlight,* which won **six awards**.

Choose your favorite retailer (available in eBook or print: about 178 pages)

https://books2read.com/GodsLight

eBook ISBN: 979-8201460877 ASIN: B098W6LHVM ~ Print ISBN: 979-8223389231

Understand the direct benefits to *you* from Christ's death and resurrection.

There are seven (plus one) directly stated benefits in Scripture.

Ponder ten additional benefits resulting from the Cross.

Choose your favorite retailer (available in eBook or print: about 206 pages)

https://books2read.com/ChristsBlood

eBook ISBN: 979-8201564209 ASIN: B0BCPN5YGW ~ Print ISBN: 979-8223331643

Everyone is tempted (even Christ was)

50+ practical tips for personal victory over temptation!

Understand the battle and your spiritual weapons

Overcome the types of temptations you will face

Be confident and victorious in your Christian life

Choose your favorite retailer (available in eBook or print: about 228 pages)

https://books2read.com/temptation-50tips

eBook ISBN: 979-8201002053 ASIN: B09SGSQLH9 ~ Print ISBN: 979-8223938781

Achieve a more consistent Christian life

As humans, we all have a common problem. Like rust to steel, pride is to our lives. Although there are examples of good pride in the Bible, most of the time pride is a negative part of our being.

Understanding the problem of pride is a vital part of gaining consistent spiritual victory as we live our daily lives.

Choose your favorite retailer (available in eBook or print: about 158 pages)

https://books2read.com/Pride-Good-and-Bad

eBook ISBN: 979-8215866122 ASIN: B0BSZZSY8J ~ Print ISBN: 979-8223612964

The Biblical account of Samson's life includes ten significant victories interspersed among fifteen problematic events. How can we avoid a spiritually fickle life? What are the commonalities and contrasts between the lives of Samson and Christ? How did God evaluate Samson's life?

What practical lessons can we apply to our daily activities by looking at his life?

Choose your favorite retailer (available in eBook or Print: about 240 pages).

https://www.booksrlr.com/ebooks/samson/

eBook ISBN: 979-8223422327 ASIN: B0CBBC7DZC ~ Print ISBN: 979-8223315902

Follow Peter's life in chronological order as he progresses from a fickle follower to a dynamic disciple. This book can easily be a *fast read*. Due to small segments, it can also be used for *daily devotions* or in *short segments* by busy individuals. For scholars it can be the basis for a *lengthy personal study*. Small groups use it as a *spur to discussions*. Whatever your choice, enjoy as you read and reflect!

Choose your favorite retailer (available in eBook or Print: about 370 pages).

https://www.booksrlr.com/ebooks/peter-failure-to-faith/

eBook ISBN: 979-8224095773 ASIN: B0D1RCQF5X ~ Print ISBN: 979-8224601868

Joseph's life illustrates many important life principles for us today. No matter what your past, like Joseph you can accomplish great things for God in the future. You too can choose to use your past tribulations for future triumphs. The author follows Joseph's life chronologically through the Bible and shows similarities with the life of Jesus. Guidelines are provided for a fast read, a moderate read, and a slow read.

Choose your favorite retailer (available in eBook or Print: about 790 pages).

https://www.booksrlr.com/ebooks-or-print/joseph-victim-to-victor/

eBook ISBN: 978-1393887959 ASIN: B088FZ3XSC ~ Print ISBN: 979-8223787563

Note: This eBook is an updated and significantly expanded version of an earlier print book "*JIM ELLIOT: A Christian Martyr Speaks to You.*"

Jim Elliot's spoken words transcribed for you – six practical messages with amazing depth and insight. These messages were given by this martyred Christian missionary before he left for the mission field in Ecuador. They were transcribed from a wire recorder, a forerunner of the magnetic tape recorder.

Christians of all maturity levels benefit from the understanding gained from Jim's discussions.

Choose your favorite retailer (available in eBook or print: about 204 pages)

https://books2read.com/JimElliot

Print Book: ISBN: 978-0741475534 ~ "***GOD LIGHT: Sunlight Sonlight***" <u>won six awards</u> and is an easy-to-read devotional style book which presents new and unforgettable insights. This book identifies fascinating parallels between natural and spiritual light, and provides applications of natural and spiritual light. Analogies teach profound truth in simple language.

Available wherever quality print books are sold.

Note: There is an eBook update of the first two sections of this book entitled: "*GOD'S NATURE: Sonlight Sunlight.*" The third section of this book is updated in the eBook entitled: "*GOD'S LIGHT: How To Respond.*" Both are listed previously.

Print Book: ISBN: 978-0741462329 ~ ***ONE PRECIOUS PEARL: God's Design for His Church*** <u>won five awards.</u>

A straightforward look at the three most common interpretations of this parable.

The major portion of the book provides parallels between the "one pearl of great price" and the Christian Church.

Available wherever quality print books are sold.

Note: There is an eBook update of this book is entitled "*GOD'S CHURCH: Christ's Pearl.*" It is listed previously.

Print Book: ISBN: 978-1606474310 ~ *"THY WILL BE DONE ON EARTH: Understanding God's Will* **for** *You"* is for those who are serious about living life in a way that pleases God.

Through the development of two graphic models the author provides insights regarding the interrelationship of fundamentals of the Christian faith.

Available wherever quality print books are sold.

Note: There is an eBook update of this book entitled *"GOD'S DESIRE: How To Please God."* It is listed previously.

Print Book: ISBN: 978-1615797646 ~ *"JIM ELLIOT: A Christian Martyr Speaks To You"* is directly relevant to all Christians.

Those with an interest in the history of missions or current missions will find the book riveting.

All Christians will appreciate Jim's straightforward, hard-hitting style of speaking.

Available wherever quality print books are sold.

Note: There is an eBook update of this book entitled *"JIM ELLIOT: Recorded Messages."* It has been enhanced and expanded with two additional messages and is listed previously.

[1] Chapter 2 shows a variety of descriptions of Israel's downward cycles.

[2] *Stepping Up: A Call to Courageous Manhood;* Dennis Rainey

[3] *"This 3,100-Year-Old Inscription May Be Linked to a Biblical Judge"*; Livia Gershon, Daily Correspondent, July 13, 2021; https://www.smithsonianmag.com/smart-news/3000-year-old-jug-holds-name-biblical-judge-180978159/

[4] MacMillan Bible Atlas

[5] In the King James or "Authorized Version'

[6] Strong's Concordance #H1439

[7] Brown-Driver-Briggs Hebrew Definitions

[8] Clarke

[9] Cundall

[10] Clarke

[11] A.W. Tozer

[12] Philosopher Cornelius Plantinga

[13] Keil and Delitzsch Biblical Commentary on the Old Testament

[14] Some have attributed this to Selina Hastings of Huntingdon (1707-1791) who reportedly said "I owe my salvation to the letter "m".

[15] John D. Barry; "Ascent of Heres;"[1] *The Lexham Bible Dictionary*; Lexham Press,; Bellingham, WA; 2016.

[16] Not all Bible translations include the mention of the position of the sun, in addition to Young's Literal Translation quoted here other translation that do include

---

1. https://ref.ly/logosres/lbd?hw=Ascent+of+Heres

the sun include Douay-Rheims, King James Version, Literal Standard, Webster's Bible Translation, and others).

[17] Albert Barnes" *Notes on Bible Books*, op. cit., p. 437.

[18] Albert Barnes: *Notes on the Old Testament: Exodus to Ruth*; ed. F. C. Cook and J. M. Fuller (London: John Murray, 1879), 437.

[19] J. R. Dummelow, editor; *A Commentary on the Holy Bible*; New York; The Macmillan Company; 1936; page 165.

Don't miss out!

Visit the website below and you can sign up to receive emails whenever Robert Lloyd Russell publishes a new book. There's no charge and no obligation.

https://books2read.com/r/B-A-QQUI-PTKZE

BOOKS 2 READ

Connecting independent readers to independent writers.

Also by Robert Lloyd Russell

Bible Character Series
Samson: Spirit-Controlled to Self-Centered
Peter: Failure to Faith
Joseph: Victim to Victor
Gideon: Wimp to Warrior

Christian Concepts Series
God's Church: Christ's Pearl
God's Nature: Sonlight Sunlight
God's Child: Like a Tree

Christian Growth Series
God's Desire: How To Please God
God's Light: How To Respond
Christ's Disciple: How To Finish Strong

Christian Theology Series
Christ's Blood: 7+ Amazing Benefits

Pride: Good and Bad

Temptation: 50+ Tips

Missions

Jim Elliot: Recorded Messages

Watch for more at www.booksrlr.com.